Queen
ELIZABETH II's
⮞GUIDE *to* LIFE⮜

Also by Karen Dolby

The Wicked Wit of Queen Elizabeth II
The Wicked Wit of Prince Philip
The Wicked Wit of Princess Margaret

Queen ELIZABETH II's ≈GUIDE *to* LIFE≈

Compiled by

KAREN DOLBY

Michael O'Mara Books Limited

First published in Great Britain in 2019 by
Michael O'Mara Books Limited
9 Lion Yard
Tremadoc Road
London SW4 7NQ

A CIP catalogue record for this book is available from the
British Library.

Papers used by Michael O'Mara Books Limited are natural,
recyclable products made from wood grown in sustainable forests.
The manufacturing processes conform to the environmental
regulations of the country of origin.

ISBN: 978-1-78929-176-6 in hardback print format
ISBN: 978-1-78929-178-0 in ebook format

1 2 3 4 5 6 7 8 9 10

Designed and typeset by K.DESIGN, Winscombe, Somerset
Printed and bound by CPI Group (UK) Ltd, Croydon CR0 4YY
www.mombooks.com

Contents

Introduction

For many people, Queen Elizabeth II quite simply *is* the monarchy, the personification of what royalty means in the modern world. She has reigned for longer than any other monarch in British history and since her first overseas trip to South Africa in 1947, she has visited over 120 countries, clocking up well over a million miles and circumnavigating the globe on a number of occasions. She has also travelled the length and breadth of the United Kingdom. The absolute model of diplomacy, she has acted as ambassador and states-woman, as well as being the face of Great Britain. She has met with heads of state and the general public, at ease with both, combining the pomp and pageantry of centuries-old traditions with a genuine warmth and personal touch. One of the most famous women in the world, at heart she is a mother and grandmother who loves the outdoors, her horses and dogs, and welcomes a good gossip as 'a wonderful tonic'.

Quietly authoritative, the Queen on duty makes it all look very easy, but it wasn't always so. Until the age of ten, when her uncle King Edward VIII abdicated, she had never expected to be the Sovereign. Then her father's early death meant Elizabeth ascended the throne before her 26th birthday. It was a steep learning curve for the naturally modest and rather shy Princess, whose early ambition was to 'marry a farmer' and have 'lots of cows, horses and children'. Despite her youth, elder statesmen such as Winston Churchill and Harold Macmillan were struck by her assurance and poise. She had a good memory and a keen eye for detail. She learned quickly. Sir Alan 'Tommy' Lascelles, her first Private Secretary after she became Queen, reflected that 'People will not realize for years how intelligent she is … Eventually it will become an accepted national fact.'

During her long reign of sixty-seven years and counting, the country and the world have changed beyond all recognition. Queen Elizabeth II has remained a constant. She once commented, 'I am the last bastion of standards.' But she has also had to learn how to navigate the new order, to embrace the best of the modern while holding on to 'fundamental principles' and 'ageless ideals'.

The Queen is in a unique position. Under her stewardship, the monarchy has adapted and evolved. She inherited her title and role when Britain was still in the grip of post-war rationing and austerity. Now into a new millennium, at the age of ninety-three the Queen is still working, still doing her duty, undoubtedly a career woman and one of the most recognizable world leaders.

Straightforward, practical, courageous, formidable and dignified are just a few of the adjectives most often used to describe the Monarch. The broad smile and twinkling eyes also suggest a sharp sense of humour, a quality most often reserved for family and friends, but increasingly apparent in public. This book looks at the character traits and values that have affected her approach to life, as well as the events and relationships that have helped to shape her reign.

1

A Sense of Duty

On 6 February 1952, twenty-five-year-old Princess Elizabeth became Queen on the death of her father, King George VI. Although his health had been steadily worsening, at just fifty-six years of age his death took the country by surprise. Six days earlier he had waved his daughter and her husband off from London Airport (later known as Heathrow); they were taking his place on a long-planned royal tour of East Africa, Australia and New Zealand. The royal party went to Kenya first and were based at Sagana Lodge, just north of Nairobi, which was a wedding present to the Royal Couple from the Kenyan people. They stayed one night at Treetops, a large treehouse built in a giant fig tree in Aberdare National Park, where they spent a memorable afternoon and evening watching wildlife from their unique vantage point. It was during their stay at Treetops that the King died, but the new Queen would not receive word until the next day, back at Sagana Lodge.

Prince Philip was told first and it was he who broke the news to his wife. Later, her cousin Lady Pamela Mountbatten went to comfort her: 'In her usual extraordinary way … she was thinking about what everybody else was having to do. Typically, she said, "Oh, thank you. But I am so sorry it means we have to go back to England and it's upsetting everybody's plans."'

What's in a Name?

One of the first questions to be raised after the King's death concerned the name that the new Queen wanted to use, which is not such an odd enquiry when you are royal. Indeed, her father's first name was Albert – family and friends generally called him Bertie – and George was actually his fourth name.

Before the royal party left Kenya, her Private Secretary Martin Charteris had asked, 'What are you going to call yourself?' Elizabeth replied immediately, 'My own name, of course. What else?' It was agreed that she should become Queen Elizabeth II, following on from the Tudor monarch Elizabeth I and to distinguish her from Queen Elizabeth the Queen Mother.

A New Elizabethan Era

Barely a week after leaving the UK, the new Queen arrived back at London Airport on the evening of 7 February. A sombre party descended the steps to be met by Prime Minister Winston Churchill, Foreign Secretary Anthony Eden, Leader of the Opposition Clement Attlee and other senior politicians.

Later at Clarence House, her eighty-four-year-old grand-mother Queen Mary curtseyed and kissed her hand in a reversal of their usual roles, although the dowager queen couldn't help adding, 'Lilibet, your skirts are much too short for mourning.'

The next day, Queen Elizabeth II held her first Privy Council at St James's Palace, at which she read her Accession Declaration:

> By the sudden death of my dear Father, I am called to assume the duties and responsibilities of Sovereignty … My heart is too full for me to say more to you today than that I shall always work, as my Father did throughout his Reign, to uphold constitutional government and to advance the happiness and prosperity of my Peoples … I pray that God will help me to discharge worthily this heavy task that has been lain upon me so early in my life.

Privately, the Queen Mother wrote to Queen Mary, 'I cannot bear to think of Lilibet, so young to bear such a burden.'

She was not the only one to worry about the Queen's youth. The Prime Minister fretted that he did not know the new Queen and that she was still hardly more than a child. But Churchill soon realized he had underestimated the young Monarch.

According to Martin Charteris, 'He was impressed by her. She was conscientious, she was well informed, she was serious-minded. Within days of her Accession she was receiving prime ministers and presidents, ambassadors and high commissioners … and doing so faultlessly.'

Looking back on this time in her life some forty years later, the Queen reflected, 'It was all very sudden … taking it on and making the best job you can. It's a question of maturing into something that one's got used to doing, and accepting the fact that here you are, and it's your fate, because I think continuity is important.'

The Coronation

Although she became Queen at the moment of her father's death, Elizabeth was not crowned or invested with the regalia of Sovereignty until the Coronation at Westminster Abbey. This formal ceremony usually takes place some months after the death of the previous monarch, to allow for a period of mourning, but in this instance it was decided to delay the event for sixteen months to allow enough time for the elaborate preparations.

Westminster Abbey was closed to the public from 1 January 1953 and for the next five months the building was adapted to accommodate thousands of guests and also television cameras, as a decision had been made to film the service, with the exception of the anointing. John Brooke-Little, who was a member of the Earl Marshal's Coronation staff, explained, 'There was an awful lot to do, because, after all, there hadn't been a Coronation of a married sovereign since Queen Anne. There weren't many precedents ... We had such things as television to cope with, and the whole Abbey had to be turned into a sort of theatre.'

On 2 June 1953, more than 8,000 guests packed into Westminster Abbey for the Coronation, while out of a population of 36 million in the UK, it's estimated that 27 million people watched on television sets, often bought especially for the occasion, and 11 million more listened to the radio broadcast. The ceremony was also watched and listened to by millions more worldwide. *The Times* reported: 'Then the Queen came, a young and gracious figure, with her hands clasped motionless in front of her and with a smile to acknowledge the homage of curtseys and bows. She walked lightly and in slow state, her head held high, and passed, the complete Queen, to her consecration.'

Later, after the pomp and ceremony, there was a huge sense of relief back at Buckingham Palace. 'We were all running down the corridor and we all sat on a sofa together,' said Anne Glenconner, one of six specially chosen Coronation Maids of Honour, remembering the relaxed atmosphere. 'The Queen said, "Oh, that was marvellous. Nothing went wrong!" We were all laughing.'

Outside, the day drew to a close with fireworks and dancing in the streets. There was also a radio broadcast from Prime Minister Winston Churchill: 'We have had a day which the oldest of us are proud to have lived to see and which the youngest will remember all their lives.'

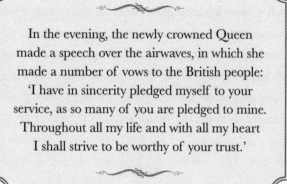

In the evening, the newly crowned Queen made a speech over the airwaves, in which she made a number of vows to the British people: 'I have in sincerity pledged myself to your service, as so many of you are pledged to mine. Throughout all my life and with all my heart I shall strive to be worthy of your trust.'

A Lifetime Commitment

Early in her reign, the young Elizabeth confided to the Dean of Windsor, 'My father told me I must always remember that whatever I said, or did, to anyone, they would remember it.' Even as a Princess she was aware of her duty and was determined to perform it to the very best of her ability. She knew that hers was a full-time commitment, a job for life. If she needed reminding, there is the full version of her title alone, 'Her Majesty Elizabeth the Second, by the Grace of God, of the United Kingdom of Great Britain and Northern Ireland, and of Her Other Realms and Territories Queen, Head of the Commonwealth, Defender of the Faith', which is more than enough to live up to.

At the Thanksgiving Service held at St Paul's Cathedral to mark her Silver Jubilee in June 1977, the Queen reaffirmed one of the promises she had made in her younger days: 'When I was twenty-one, I pledged my life to the service of our people and I asked for God's help to make good that vow. Although that vow was made in my salad days, when I was still green in judgement, I do not regret nor retract one word of it.'

When asked who was the most impressive person he had ever met, the former Prime Minister of New Zealand Sir John Key had no hesitation before answering, 'The Queen'. His reason? 'What you see is what you get. Equally, she really is a tireless worker. When you are Prime Minister, you work horrendous hours but you are elected to do that. When your time is over, it really is over … For the Queen, it's a lifetime of dedication. It's a lifetime of service.'

A long-time friend reflecting on the character of the Monarch commented, 'She is never, you know, not the Queen.'

A Grandmother's Wisdom

Queen Mary played a crucial role in both her granddaughters' education, taking Elizabeth and her younger sister Margaret on cultural visits to museums and galleries. She suggested more challenging reading material for them and encouraged the young Princesses to learn poetry by heart as 'wonderful memory training'. This has stood Elizabeth in good stead throughout her life. Princess Margaret later confessed that she found her stern and formal grandmother 'absolutely terrifying' and objected to her insistence on strict royal protocol, which meant that the Princesses were required to curtsey to their grandmother every time they met her.

Deborah Mitford, the Duchess of Devonshire, recalled that 'Queen Mary wore tiaras like she wore her toques, as if they were part of her being.' And, indeed, Queen Mary wore a tiara every evening for dinner, even if there were no guests.

Princess Margaret might have found her grandmother challenging, but Elizabeth took her lessons to heart. It was Queen Mary who suggested that it was inappropriate for a Sovereign to smile in public and who made a virtue of hiding her emotions. Although traditional in the extreme, the dowager Queen was surprisingly open to new theories and ideas, and had a passion for history, all of which she passed on to Elizabeth, who was bright, even-tempered and eager to learn.

'History is as important to these children as arithmetic,' Queen Mary instructed the Princesses' governess, Marion Crawford. 'They are not like other children.' Nevertheless, when the young Elizabeth referred to 'all the people who'll be waiting to see us outside' at a concert they were attending, her grandmother arranged for her to be taken straight home as punishment for her apparent self-importance. She emphasized that duty must always come first, and in her granddaughter and heir to the throne, Queen Mary would find someone as hardworking, dedicated and focused as herself.

Queen Mary never had any doubts about her eldest granddaughter's capabilities, recognizing her loyal, unwavering character and quietly resolute nature, and realizing that the calm exterior masked the firm commitment of one who knew her own mind. It was this which convinced Queen Mary that Princess Elizabeth was mature enough at the age of 20 to make a decision about the man she would marry: 'She won't give her heart lightly, but when she does it will be for always. It does sometimes happen that one falls in love early, and it lasts for ever. Elizabeth seems to me that kind of girl. She would always know her own mind. There's something very steadfast and determined in her – like her father.'

Partner for Life

Princess Elizabeth fell in love with eighteen-year-old Prince Philip of Greece when she was just thirteen and he was a dashing young naval cadet. Her cousin Margaret Rhodes wrote, 'She never looked at anyone else.' The couple were married eight years later in November 1947.

In her choice of husband and consort, Elizabeth found the perfect partner. Prince Philip stood beside her at every important occasion and state visit for almost seventy years, performing his duty with great dignity until his final solo public engagement in August 2017 and subsequent retirement at the age of ninety-six. Shortly after his wife became Queen, the Prince explained to his first Private Secretary, Michael Parker, 'My job, first, second and last, is never to let the Queen down.' At the Coronation, the Prince was the first to pay homage, promising, 'I, Philip, Duke of Edinburgh, do become your liege man of life and limb,' and he has fulfilled this oath ever since.

> When asked what he would like to be remembered for as he approached his ninetieth birthday, Prince Philip was at a loss. As far as he was concerned, he'd just done his duty. 'I doubt I've achieved anything likely to be remembered.'

In December 2000, he expanded on his role when speaking to American journalists at a press lunch in London: 'I'm, I suppose, a pragmatist. I mean, I'm here, and I might as well get on with it. There's no good saying "what if" all the time. You can't go round all your life envying other people or wishing you were doing something else.'

For her part, the Queen paid tribute to her husband's sense of duty at a lunch held at Banqueting House in Whitehall, to mark their Golden Wedding anniversary on 20 November 1997: 'He is someone who doesn't take easily to compliments, but he has, quite simply, been my strength and stay all these years, and I, and his whole family, and this and many other countries, owe him a debt greater than he would ever claim or we shall ever know.'

An Array of Royal Duties

Every day, with the exceptions of Christmas and Easter, wherever she is in the country or the world the Queen attends to her red-leather dispatch boxes containing official government papers. In the earlier years of her reign her second Private Secretary, Sir Michael Adeane, calculated that she spent at least three hours every day conscientiously reading through papers and sometimes worked late into the evening. Staying with friends one weekend, the Queen explained, 'I must do my boxes. If I missed one once, I would never get it straight again.'

The Queen also insisted on looking at correspondence from the public, saying that she saw them as 'rather personal to oneself, that people write them thinking that I'm going to open them and read them'. The letters provide her with an insight and 'give one an idea of what is worrying people'.

At an investiture ceremony, the Queen was particularly impressed by a soldier to whom she was giving an award for gallantry. When she commended him for his bravery, he answered simply, 'It was just the training.' Reflecting on this, she replied, 'I have a feeling that in the end, probably, the training is the answer to a great many things. You can do a lot if you're properly trained. And I hope I have been.'

During a Royal Tour of Nigeria in February 1956, the Queen and Prince Philip visited the Oji River leper settlement near Enugu, at a time when anyone suffering from leprosy was still treated as an outcast, even those who had been cured. The Queen listened to speeches and shook hands with former sufferers prompting journalist Barbara Ward to write, 'Qualities of grace and compassion shine through the spectacle of a young queen shaking hands with cured Nigerian lepers to reassure timid villagers who do not believe in the cure.'

The Queen has been a member of the Sandringham branch of the Women's Institute since 1943 and speaking in January 2019, after unveiling the branch's centenary plaque, she said, 'As we look for new answers in the modern age, I for one prefer the tried and tested recipes, like speaking well of each other and respecting different points of view; coming together to seek out the common ground; and never losing sight of the bigger picture.'

Above the Law

As Monarch, there are various rules that simply do not apply. All members of the Royal Family are exempt from the Freedom of Information Act, but the Queen is the only person in the world who does not need a passport in order to travel. As passports are issued in her name, it is simply unnecessary for her to carry one. She doesn't need an ID card or a driving licence either, a perk which also applies only to the Queen.

Although the law of the land applies to the Queen, it does not allow her to be prosecuted – 'civil and criminal proceedings cannot be taken against the Sovereign as a person under UK law'. Effectively, the Queen could literally get away with murder. Fortunately, she does not need reminding that with great power comes great responsibility and the official royal website states, 'The Queen is careful to ensure that all her activities in her personal capacity are carried out in strict accordance with the law.'

Drive Time

As well as not being required to hold a driving licence in order to drive, the Queen is also not obliged to have number plates on her cars, although her personal (rather than state) vehicles usually do. However, Her Majesty knows how to change a flat tyre and service a car or lorry following her time in the Auxiliary Territorial Service (ATS) during the Second World War. So enamoured was the Princess with her new-found skills as a mechanic that she must have conveyed her enthusiasm to the family at home, as her mother once commented drily, 'We had sparking plugs all the way through dinner.'

Princess Elizabeth joined the ATS in spring 1944 as a Second Subaltern and as part of her training she learned to drive. Her Company Commander described her as 'a very good and extremely careful and considerate driver'.

That's not quite how members of her family have described the Queen's driving in more recent years. Her cousin Margaret Rhodes is not the only person to have said that she drives 'like a bat out of hell'. She also never wears a seatbelt. Although protocol dictates that she is chauffeured when travelling to public engagements, the Queen used to enjoy driving herself to private functions, particularly when staying at Balmoral and Sandringham, or one of her other country estates. Visitors to Windsor Great Park were sometimes surprised by a glimpse of the racing royal speeding past.

The Queen took a gleeful delight in telling Sir Sherard Cowper-Coles, who in 2003 was the newly appointed British Ambassador to Saudi Arabia, the story of how she had once terrified the late King Abdullah of Saudi Arabia in 1998. It was during the then Crown Prince's first visit to Balmoral and after lunch he expressed an interest in seeing the Scottish estate. Land Rovers were duly brought round to the front of the castle and Prince Abdullah was rather taken aback to find the Sovereign herself behind the wheel as his driver and tour guide. The Queen roared off, accelerating fast. Seemingly oblivious to her passenger's discomfort, the Queen chatted all the way, pointing out landmarks, taking her hands off the wheel and navigating the narrow estate roads at speed. Speaking through his interpreter, Prince Abdullah begged the Queen to slow down. She carried on regardless. Maybe out of solidarity with all the Saudi women, who at the time were not allowed to drive, or maybe because it was her private estate, her car and the fact she loves driving, and that even the most sensible Sovereign needs to let off steam sometimes.

Following on from Prince Philip's decision to surrender his licence and stop driving, shortly after his accident near their Sandringham home in January 2019, there are suggestions that the Queen has also decided, probably reluctantly, that at the age of ninety-three it may be time for her to give up driving on public roads.

Out and About

It's hard to imagine a time when members of the Royal Family did not meet and greet the public, but it was Queen Elizabeth II who broke with tradition to make it the norm. During a state tour of Australia and New Zealand with

Prince Philip in 1970, she suggested that instead of meeting only with officials, she also wanted an opportunity to talk to ordinary people in the crowd. The experiment was a big success. The 'walkabout', as it was immediately christened, has remained a feature of royal visits at home and abroad ever since.

Other members of the Royal Family, however, were less convinced by the new practice in the early days. The Queen's daughter, Princess Anne, was not a fan originally. She does not have fond memories of her first experiences: 'A nineteen-year-old suddenly being dropped in the middle of the street and being told to pick someone and talk to them. Fun? No, I don't think so. A challenge.'

The younger generation of Princes and their wives are more enthusiastic. Kate, the Duchess of Cambridge, obviously enjoys meeting the public and has confessed, 'There's a real art to walkabouts. Everybody teases me in the family that I spend far too long chatting. I still have to learn a little bit more and pick up a few more tips, I suppose.'

All in a Day's Work

At an engagement in Lanarkshire, Scotland, the royal car approached the line of people ready to greet the Queen and her party. The Queen stepped out and looked back to see where her Lord-Lieutenant had got to, as he was due to handle formalities and make introductions. Unfortunately, Lord Clydesmuir was struggling to extricate himself from the car, his long ceremonial sword proving something of a problem. As the situation was taking so long to be resolved, the Queen decided to take control and go it alone. Advancing on the waiting line, she said, 'My Lord-Lieutenant appears to be having difficulty in getting out of the car, so I'd better introduce myself. I'm the Queen.'

Every year the Queen invites the twenty-four Knights and other royal members of the Order of the Garter to Garter Day, where they have lunch at Windsor Castle and then attend a service in St George's Chapel. It's a historic occasion with origins dating back to 1348 and everyone dons ceremonial blue velvet robes and wide-brimmed feathered hats. As Garter Day takes place in June, it is often swelteringly hot in the heavy attire. 'Whoever invented these robes … they're not really very practical,' the Queen has commented. 'They couldn't have been practical even in the days when somebody wore clothes like this.'

The Queen has ensured there is at least one concession to practicality. The Members of the Garter always walk down the hill to the chapel and then take carriages and cars back up. As the Queen reasoned, 'It's always very lucky to plod downhill and not uphill.'

A Fan of Popular Culture

The Queen has visited the sets of a number of popular television shows and soaps over the years. One of her most recent was a tour of the *Game of Thrones* set in Belfast. While there she saw the infamous Iron Throne, but declined the chance to try it out, saying, 'It looks rather uncomfortable.'

She and Prince Philip obviously watch the BBC's satirical news show *Have I Got News For You*. Speaking at the Hay Literary Festival in 2016, actor Brian Blessed told the story of a conversation he had with the Queen shortly after he had hosted the programme. She referred in particular to the story he had told about climbing Mount Everest and some of the more basic challenges he had to face, as well as his use of the bleeped out f-word. 'The Queen was in hysterics about it,' Blessed explained. '[She said] that was a funny story you told about going to the toilet on Everest, Mr Blessed. What I would like to say to you is that the word f**k is an Anglo-Saxon word. It means spreading the seed.'

Brian Blessed also revealed that Her Majesty
was a fan of *Flash Gordon* and that she had told
him, 'We watch *Flash Gordon* all the time …
with the children and grandchildren,' before
asking him, 'Would you mind saying "Gordon's
alive"?' The actor was happy to oblige.

Fundamental Principles

It was under Prince Philip's direction that cameras were
allowed into Westminster Abbey to televise the Coronation,
but the Queen remained very wary in the early days of her
reign. Writing to former Prime Minister Anthony Eden
before her US trip in October 1957, she said, 'Television is
the worst of all, but I suppose when one gets used to it, it is
not so terrible as at first sight.'

This was also the year that she had decided to make her
annual Christmas broadcast on television for the first time
rather than on radio. The Queen practised reading rolling
type on a teleprompter as well as studying an instructional
film produced by a BBC announcer, but despite her preparations she was nervous, confessing, 'My husband seems to

have found the secret of how to relax on television. I am still worried because I have not found the secret yet.'

She began her historic broadcast from the Long Library at Sandringham by saying, 'Twenty-five years ago my grandfather broadcast the first of these Christmas messages. Today is another landmark ...' She continued, 'I very much hope that this new medium will make my Christmas message more personal and direct. It is inevitable that I should seem a rather remote figure to many of you. A successor to the kings and queens of history; someone whose face may be familiar in newspapers and films but who never really touches your personal lives. But now at least for a few minutes I welcome you to the peace of my own home.'

The Queen went on to acknowledge the nature and pace of developments throughout the world: 'That it is possible for some of you to see me today is just another example of the speed at which things are changing all around us. Because of these changes I am not surprised that many people feel lost and unable to decide what to hold on to and what to discard. How to take advantage of the new life without losing the best of the old. But it is not the new inventions which are the difficulty. The trouble is caused by unthinking people who carelessly throw away ageless ideals as if they were old and outworn machinery.'

In order to hold onto 'fundamental principles', she called for a 'special kind of courage ... which makes us stand up for everything that we know is right, everything that is true and honest. We need the kind of courage that can withstand the subtle corruption of the cynics so that we can show the world that we are not afraid of the future.

'It has always been easy to hate and destroy. To build and to cherish is much more difficult ... I cannot lead you into battle, I do not give you laws or administer justice but I can do something else. I can give you my heart and my devotion to these old islands and to all the peoples of our brotherhood of nations.'

The Queen had no need to worry. An estimated 30 million people watched and the broadcast was a huge success. the *Daily Express* praised 'her charm, grace and simplicity', and *The New York Times* described her performance as 'unstrained and natural'.

A Disciplined Approach

Like her great-great-grandmother Victoria, the Queen has always kept a daily diary. She has described it as 'my secret friend', and commented that writing in it was 'just like scrubbing your teeth'. Friends have speculated that it may contain some of her more sharply humorous observations, but the contents will not be made public until long after her death. The Queen is typically modest about her writing saying, 'It's not really a diary like Queen Victoria's, you know … or as detailed as that. It's quite small.'

Embracing the New

The Queen sent her first email way back in 1976 and was the first head of state to do so. It was sent on 26 March during a visit to the Royal Signals and Radar Establishment in Malvern. This was part of a demonstration of networking technology called Arpanet and predated the invention of the internet as we know it. Her username was HME2 and the email was entitled: 'Text of message to be transmitted by Her Majesty the Queen.'

In October 2014, Queen Elizabeth II sent her first tweet from the Science Museum in London, keeping it simply informative: 'It is a pleasure to open the Information Age exhibition today at the @ScienceMuseum and I hope people will enjoy visiting. Elizabeth R.'

The Queen had previously joined social media in November 2010 with a Facebook page called 'The British Monarchy' and the Royal Family's official Twitter account was created in April 2009 to share royal news and engagements. At that time it was announced that 'no members of the Royal Family would be tweeting'.

She went on to make her first Instagram post on the Royal

Family account in March 2019. This was also at the Science Museum, where she used an iPad to share an image of a two-page letter written by Charles Babbage, the world's first computer pioneer, to her great-great-grandfather Prince Albert.

The Queen may have embraced social media, but there are some aspects of twenty-first-century life that Her Majesty is less keen on. Presenting himself at Buckingham Palace when he first became US Ambassador to the UK in 2013, Matthew Barzun referred to the crowds who had photographed him as he drove through the London streets in the Queen's horse-drawn carriage. The Queen looked thoughtful, 'There've always been tourists and they always used to have regular cameras. They'd put them up, take a picture and then put them down. Now' – at this point she held her hand over her face – 'they put these things up and they never take them down. And I miss seeing their eyes.'

There has been one national craze that no one could have predicted Her Majesty would join in with. In a year when photo-bombing became something of an obsession, a young

Australian hockey player named Jayde Taylor paused to take a selfie with her teammate Brooke Peris at the 2014 Commonwealth Games in Glasgow. As they posed for the camera, in the background stood the Queen, smiling broadly, dressed in green, complete with feathered hat. She was obviously completely aware of what she was doing and thoroughly enjoying the joke.

And that isn't the only occasion when the Queen has dabbled with photo-bombing. A year earlier, during a live BBC news programme at Broadcasting House in London, the two presenters were surprised to discover Her Majesty approaching the glass screen that separated them from the busy newsroom behind. Clad in brilliant turquoise, the Queen took centre stage surrounded by BBC staff keen to follow the royal progress. Meanwhile, the presenters struggled to regain their composure and control of the programme.

God Save Our Gracious Queen

There are times when duty is mixed with fun and as the years have passed, there is a sense that the Monarch increasingly relishes these occasions.

When director Danny Boyle came up with the idea for a James Bond sketch as part of the opening ceremony for the

London 2012 Olympic Games, he pitched it as an original way to introduce both the Sovereign and the national anthem. They anticipated finding an actress to play the part of the Queen and wrote to the Palace to ask for permission, as protocol dictates. Boyle explained that, to their amazement, 'They came back and said, "We're delighted for you to do it, and Her Majesty would like to be in it herself," and the surreal thing, "she would like to play herself".'

When it came to filming, it was the Queen who suggested she should say something and who came up with the lines. 'We started shooting and she turned round and she said her lines beautifully,' the director reported.

The Queen's role in the ceremony was so secret that even Princes Charles, William and Harry knew nothing about it. They joined everyone else in watching open-mouthed with surprise, before roaring with appreciative laughter. The sketch was such a success that it has been used as the basis for a number of spoof versions since.

2
Family Values

Queen Elizabeth has four children: Prince Charles, Princess Anne, Prince Andrew and Prince Edward; eight grandchildren: Peter Phillips, Zara Tindall, Prince William, Prince Harry, Princess Beatrice, Princess Eugenie, Lady Louise Windsor and James, Viscount Severn; and, to date, eight great-grandchildren: Savannah Phillips, Isla Phillips, Prince George, Mia Tindall, Princess Charlotte, Prince Louis, Lena Tindall and Archie Harrison Mountbatten-Windsor.

As Great Britain's most famous great-grandmother, it is no surprise that the Queen values family life: 'Marriage gains from the web of family relationships between parents and children, grandparents and grandchildren, cousins, aunts and uncles.'

That doesn't mean that all is plain sailing. She has also commented, 'Like all the best families, we have our share of eccentricities, of impetuous and wayward youngsters and of family disagreements.' And acknowledged more seriously that, 'Grief is the price we pay for love.'

Sisters, Sisters

As a girl, Princess Elizabeth took her role as big sister seriously. After her father became King, she saw it as her duty to set an example and help Princess Margaret to navigate the complex niceties of royal protocol.

'Now, Margaret, be sure to copy me and you will be all right,' she once advised her young sister. And before an official garden party at Buckingham Palace she was more specific: 'If you see someone with a funny hat, Margaret, you must *not* point at it and laugh. And you must *not* be in too much of a hurry to get through the crowds to the tea table. That's not polite either.'

A Royal Partnership

The Queen is the only British monarch to have celebrated her Diamond Wedding anniversary and Prince Philip is far and away the longest-serving consort of a British sovereign. Until his retirement from public duties in 2017 he had stood beside the Queen for almost seventy years, accompanying her on all her Commonwealth tours and state visits, as well as countless public engagements both at home and abroad. They make a formidable duo and there is no doubt that his support has been vital. The pair are often seen sharing a joke, laughing and chatting. After their 60th wedding anniversary on 20 November 2007, one of the Queen's advisers said of the Royal Couple, 'They are not physically demonstrative, but they have a strong connection. She still lights up when he walks into the room. She becomes softer, lighter and happier.' When apart, Prince Philip calls his wife every evening to talk over the day's events.

Biographer Sarah Bradford's verdict was that 'the Queen relies on him tremendously. Through all those troubles they certainly did get closer. They are very close. They understand each other.'

The Queen and Prince Philip were married at Westminster Abbey on 20 November 1947, following a royal tradition dating back to 1100 when King Henry I married Princess Matilda of Scotland there on 11 November. The Queen's parents, King George VI and Queen Elizabeth (then Albert, Duke of York and Lady Elizabeth Bowes-Lyon), were also married in the Abbey on 26 April 1923.

As a Royal Couple, even wedding anniversaries become public events. Speaking at their 25th wedding anniversary celebration at the Guildhall in London in 1972, the Queen poked fun at herself and one of her well-used phrases, saying, 'I think everybody really will concede that on this, of all days, I should begin my speech with the words "My husband and I".'

Royal they may be, but in many ways, the Queen and Prince Philip are like any other long-married couple.

During their lengthy Commonwealth tour in 1954, the Queen was filmed in Australia in the middle of a heated argument with her husband, 'hurling shoes and threats and sporting equipment, and venting the sort of regal fury that, in another age, would have cost someone their head,' Robert Hardman wrote. The Queen later apologized to the journalists who had witnessed the row: 'I'm sorry for that little interlude, but, as you know, it happens in every marriage.'

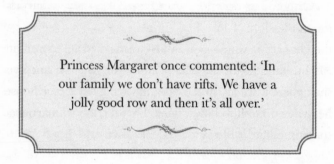

Princess Margaret once commented: 'In our family we don't have rifts. We have a jolly good row and then it's all over.'

'Yak, yak, yak. Come on, get a move on,' Prince Philip shouted to the Queen, who was still chatting to their hosts on the quayside in Belize in 1994. The Prince, meanwhile, was ready waiting on the deck of the Royal Yacht *Britannia*, impatient to depart.

Also on board *Britannia*, the Queen is reported to have said firmly, 'I'm not coming out of my cabin until he's in a better temper. I'm going to stay here on my bed until he's better.'

After watching Prince Philip down his third champagne cocktail at a reception, his wife remarked a touch frostily, 'What kind of speech do you think you are going to make now?'

On another occasion, the Queen also made a surprising confession: 'I love looking at houses, but I never get the chance. It would be too awkward to invite myself in. My husband heard me talking about this one day and ever since then, if we are in the car and we pass by a nice house, he drives up to it to have a look. I get terribly embarrassed sometimes and all I can do is duck down and hide.'

Home is Where the Heart Is

Alongside her duties as Monarch, the Queen places great importance upon her role as wife and mother, once commenting, 'Woman's paramount duty is the home. It's there she finds her truest fulfilment.'

Princess Anne once said of her mother, 'It's much more difficult to remember that she's a Queen than a mother. After all, I've known her longer as a mother than as a Queen.' She added, 'As all mothers, she's put up with a lot and we're still on speaking terms, so I think that's no mean feat.'

When they were small children, the Queen taught both Prince Charles and Princess Anne to read and tell the time using a blackboard. After she first acceded to the throne, the pressures of finding her way in a challenging new role meant she could no longer be as hands-on as a mother. By the time her grandchildren were born she could relax and enthusiastically embrace being a grandmother. This became even more important after her children's divorces. Princess Anne said of the Queen that having reached the normal parental stage 'when you think you can't get the children out of the house quickly enough … you suddenly realize how quiet it is, and I think she quite missed that part of having children, so the grandchildren were very much enjoyed, all of them.'

An investiture ceremony at Buckingham Palace on 15 November 1977 was one of the few times Her Majesty has ever been late for an engagement. She had good reason. Captain Mark Phillips had rung her with the good news that Princess Anne had had a baby boy at St Mary's Hospital, Paddington. When she arrived the Queen explained, 'I apologize for being late but I have just had a message from the hospital. My daughter has just given birth to a son.' Peter Phillips was the Queen's first grandchild.

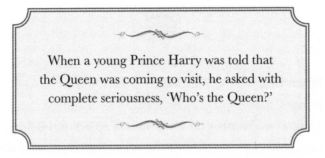

When a young Prince Harry was told that the Queen was coming to visit, he asked with complete seriousness, 'Who's the Queen?'

Royal Residences

'They say an Englishman's home is his castle. What I want is to turn my castle into a home,' the Queen has asserted.

And Her Majesty is not short of castles to choose from. Alongside state-owned Buckingham Palace and Windsor Castle, among many other residences in London and throughout the United Kingdom, the Queen privately owns Sandringham House in Norfolk and Balmoral Castle, Craigowan Lodge and Delnadamph Lodge on the Balmoral Estate in Aberdeenshire.

The Queen spent much of her youth at Windsor Castle, which is said to be the home closest to her own heart. She once commented to Princess Margaret, 'I wish I could live here for ever and ever,' to which her sister replied sceptically,

'You'd soon be bored.' The Queen simply said, 'Oh no! Nobody could possibly be bored at Windsor.'

The Queen has also praised their Sandringham Estate saying, 'Sandringham is so dear to me because it means so much to my husband.'

Sandringham is somewhere that offers the Royal Family a break from public life and duty. The Queen described it as, 'An escape place, but it is also a commercially viable bit of England. I like farming ... I like animals. I wouldn't be happy if I just had arable farming.' Perhaps reflecting her childhood ambition: 'When I grow up I will marry a farmer. I shall have lots of cows, horses and children.'

The Queen has always loved the beauty and wildness of the countryside around Balmoral, and commented that 'You can go out for miles and never see anybody. You can walk or ride ... [There are] endless possibilities.' She has also said of her Scottish home, 'It's rather nice to hibernate for a bit when one leads such a very moveable life.'

As a girl, she tramped the hills, deerstalking with her

father, and it is still a place where the family shoot and fish, enjoying relaxed picnics and barbecues in late summer. Balmoral witnesses the more exuberant side of the Queen's character, singing songs at the top of her voice, dancing reels at the annual Ghillies Ball in the castle ballroom, and taking part in satirical sketches and entertainments.

At Buckingham Palace, the Queen's work desk is surrounded by photographs of her family and pets. She favours comfortable sofas, paintings on the walls, books and vases of fresh flowers, commenting, 'I like my rooms to look really lived in.' The Queen prefers to write with a fountain pen that belonged to her father King George VI and her desk chair is upholstered with a piece of his embroidery, a sign of the attachment she has for her family legacy. For purely practical reasons, she always uses black blotting paper to prevent any unscrupulous snooping into her personal or state correspondence.

Home from Home at Sea

The Queen and Prince Philip set off for their first long Commonwealth tour in November 1953 on board SS *Gothic*. Returning almost six months later in May 1954, they sailed back along the River Thames on the newly commissioned Royal Yacht *Britannia*. From the start the vessel was a real home for the Royal Family, representing freedom and a welcome refuge from press and public.

The Royal Yacht was used for state visits and honeymoons, for transport overseas and around Britain, and provided the perfect setting for entertaining foreign dignitaries. Presidents, heads of state and other important guests have all been welcomed aboard.

Douglas Hurd, Foreign Secretary from 1989 to 1995, said, 'There was a magic about *Britannia* which had nothing to do with magnificence because she wasn't a magnificent ship.' He remembered the overseas tours on board the Yacht as the 'most pleasant' of his Foreign Office career, also commenting, 'She was a homely ship in the proper sense.'

The Queen herself saw the weeks she spent on *Britannia* at the end of the summer on the way to Balmoral as one of the few times she could be off-duty and fully relax. She told a Palace member of staff, 'I walk on at the end of a long summer season, I am absolutely exhausted and you won't see me for a couple of days … and at the end of a fortnight I can get off at Aberdeen with a spring in my heels, ready for another year.'

In 1990, when Rear Admiral Sir Robert Woodard was appointed Flag Officer Royal Yachts and Commander of *Britannia*, he went to see the Queen, who explained something of her thoughts on the role of the Yacht. 'People who know us at all know that Buckingham Palace is the office, Windsor Castle is for weekends and the occasional state thing, and Sandringham and Balmoral are for holidays. Well, they aren't what I would call holidays. For example, there are ninety people coming to stay with us at Balmoral this summer. The only holiday I get every year is from Portsmouth the long way round to Aberdeen on the Royal Yacht, when I can get up when I like and wear what I like and be completely free. And if you as Flag Officer Royal Yachts can produce the Royal Yacht for my summer holidays, that's all I ask.'

The choice of crew reflected the informal atmosphere. All were volunteer naval recruits and, as one of the officers explained, potential staff were asked only two questions at interview: 'Have you got a prison record; and have you got a sense of humour? And if they laughed at the first, there wasn't any need for the second.'

The relaxed camaraderie on board resulted in more than the occasional practical joke. Sir Robert Woodard's predecessor left him a number of instructions, including the strict rule that the Queen required her Flag Officer to wear best uniform at all times. It was, 'Complete rubbish,' Sir Robert explained. 'It was Hawaiian shirts and sandals!' When he duly appeared for duty before the Queen, dressed in his finest, she laughed heartily. 'Wool?' she teased. 'Over the eyes? Being pulled?'

Saying goodbye to *Britannia* was a huge wrench for the Queen and the rest of the family. It really had been their floating home. Every other castle or palace had been inherited along with the furnishings and decorations. It was on *Britannia* that the Queen and Prince Philip had been able to indulge their own tastes and choose everything.

At the decommissioning ceremony for *Britannia* at Portsmouth on 11 December 1997, very unusually the Queen was seen wiping away a tear, as was Princess Anne. It was one of the few occasions when the normally stoic Monarch has let her emotions get the better of her in public. They were not alone. *Britannia*'s former Chief Petty Officer Dick Field said, 'If the press had swung their cameras around, they would have caught another two thousand former Royal Yacht officers and Yachtsmen doing exactly the same thing. It was the worst day of our lives.'

Home for Christmas

Royal Family Christmases follow a traditional pattern. The celebrations usually take place at Sandringham. Like her grandfather George V, who first chose the Norfolk estate as the setting for the family Christmas, the Queen prefers its more homely atmosphere. She also has many happy memories of past Christmases spent there with her own parents and sister.

For many people, the Queen's speech is an integral part of Christmas Day festivities. Broadcast at 3 p.m. British time, not everyone may watch or take in everything she says, but we know it's there, reassuringly traditional, essential. In the Queen's Christmas broadcast of 1975, she said, 'It does matter therefore what each individual does each day. Kindness, sympathy, resolution and courteous behaviour are infectious.'

A true professional, the Queen always records her Christmas message in just one take.

Following the German tradition set by Queen Victoria and Prince Albert, presents are exchanged on Christmas Eve, set out on trestle tables immediately after afternoon tea. It is supposedly a tradition for the Royal Family to give one another joke presents. Rumoured gifts include a shower cap from Prince Harry to his grandmother emblazoned with the message, 'Ain't life a b***h?', a white leather loo seat from Princess Anne to her brother Prince Charles, which was apparently a surprising success, and a grow-your-own girlfriend kit from Kate to brother-in-law Prince Harry. The day ends with a formal black-tie dinner in the evening.

Beginning with a hearty breakfast, Christmas Day sees the Queen and other members of the family attending the morning church service at St Mary Magdalene, Sandringham. They take time to greet the members of the public who are waiting there to meet them. A traditional festive lunch awaits them back at the house, with the Christmas pudding and brandy butter served at 2 p.m., finished in time to sit down together to watch the Queen's speech.

Informal family time follows in the evening. Charades and other games have always been firm favourites and everyone takes part. The Queen is said to be an excellent mimic, but strictly for family and close friends only. Her specialities are wide-ranging but include a number of politicians and television characters, plus a convincing former Russian President Boris Yeltsin, along with several US presidents. She also performs a perfect imitation of the Aberdeenshire accent of a minister of the Church of Scotland who, saying grace before dinner one day at Balmoral, made an unfortunate choice of phrase: 'For the delicious meal we are about to receive, and for the intercourse afterwards, may the Lord make us truly thankful.'

The Royal Work Ethic

When asked about preparation for life as a royal, Prince Charles said, 'You pick it up as you go along. You watch and learn … I learned the way a monkey learns, by watching its parents.'

Sarah, Duchess of York, said of being part of 'the Firm', 'You have to think of the Royal Family as being like a brand.'

Prince Harry acknowledged that 'Within our private life and within certain other parts of our life we want to be as normal as possible … It's hard, because to a certain respect we will never be normal.' He also said, 'If you're born into it I think it's normal to feel as though you don't really want it, if that makes sense.'

Speaking about children growing up as part of the Royal Family, the Queen commented, 'Public life is not a fair burden to place upon them.' While Prince Philip explained, 'We try to keep our children out of the public eye so that they can grow up as normally as possible. But if you are really going to have a monarchy, you have got to have a family and the family's got to be in the public eye.'

But even those not born to the job and who marry into the family quickly realize that the privileges offered also bring responsibilities.

Sarah, Duchess of York, had some sage advice for her daughters Beatrice and Eugenie: 'When you're on the public stage, you must smile because nobody wants to see Princesses not smiling, not appreciating what they've got ... They've got great backgrounds. They've got a lucky life. Now, smile and show the world that it's okay ... And don't look grumpy and sulky and put your head down. That's a bore.'

The Queen and Prince Philip share the same strong work ethic which they expect the other members of the family to follow. The Prince put it succinctly, 'Never cancel an engagement. If you have a headache, take an aspirin.'

Prince Harry, along with William, Kate and now Meghan, has been increasingly involved with a range of charity projects stating, 'I'm not going to be some person in the Royal Family who just finds a lame excuse to go abroad and do all sorts of sunny holidays and whatever.'

A Royal Gift

Having not spent very much time with her prospective grand-daughter-in-law, Kate, before her engagement to William, the Queen reportedly had some concerns. She liked Kate but was worried that she had not developed her own identity nor forged a career. After graduating from St Andrew's University with a History of Art degree, Kate worked for her parents' company, a party goods supplier, for a while and then part-time as an accessories buyer for Jigsaw Junior clothes company. This led the hard-working Queen to question her work ethic.

However, on the Duke and Duchess of Cambridge's eighth wedding anniversary in 2019, there was no doubting Kate's commitment. As Sovereign, it's in the Queen's power to give some rather out-of-the-ordinary presents to mark special occasions. The Queen chose the anniversary to make Kate a Dame Grand Cross of the Royal Victorian Order, the highest seal of approval. The title is 'a personal gift of the Sovereign' to someone who has served the monarchy in a specific way. The Queen has previously awarded the honour to Camilla, Duchess of Cornwall on her seventh wedding anniversary and to Sophie, Countess of Wessex on her tenth. The Royal Victorian Order has five classes, from Member to Knight or Dame Grand Cross, and entitles recipients to wear a blue sash.

The honour is seen as a recognition of the Duchess's work as a member of the Royal Family, travelling the

Commonwealth on behalf of the Queen as well as championing her own causes, particularly relating to children's welfare and development, alongside raising awareness of mental health issues together with William and Harry. She has played an increasingly prominent role since her marriage and has joined the Queen at many national events.

A Sense of Economy

Along with a strong sense of duty and work ethic, both the Queen and Prince Philip are notably frugal in their own tastes, and have passed on their 'waste not, want not' attitude to their children.

As Princess Anne has commented, 'Economy is bred into me. I was brought up by my parents and by my nanny to believe that things were not to be wasted.' She has also referred to the family's principle of 'good old-fashioned Hanoverian housekeeping' in line with their desire to be as green and environmentally conscious as possible.

When undercover reporter Ryan Parry published his revelations about life inside the Palace after posing as a footman, the detail that captured the public imagination was the fact that at breakfast, cereals were served from no-nonsense Tupperware containers. Practical, reusable, economic.

The Queen and Prince Philip have introduced a number of green initiatives at their royal residences, including setting up hydropower turbines on the River Thames to generate electricity for Windsor Castle. Ahead of the curve in their care for the environment, Prince Philip especially has spoken openly about his concerns: 'Modern human civilization needs new resources, but there is one very important proviso – that permanent, irreversible or unacceptable levels of environmental damage must not be allowed.'

The solar panels that Prince Philip installed at Sandringham were among the first to be used in the UK and he began driving an electric van in the early 1980s.

Royal Humour

The evening after the wedding of Prince Charles and Lady Diana Spencer on 29 July 1981, the Queen's cousin, Lady Elizabeth Anson, hosted a party at Claridge's for 500 guests, including the Queen and Prince Philip. Television screens played video highlights from the elaborate wedding ceremony at St Paul's Cathedral. Relaxed, watching the footage while sipping a dry martini, the Queen suddenly exclaimed, 'Oh

Philip, do look! I'm wearing my Miss Piggy face.' This became something of a running joke within the Royal Household, and for the Queen's 60th birthday, staff gave her a card showing Miss Piggy wearing full royal regalia including a crown.

And this ability to laugh at herself is definitely a quality she shares with Prince Philip, and one they have passed on to the rest of the family.

'The most amusing point is meeting somebody and them going, "You're so not what I thought you were,"' Prince Harry remarked, when talking about people's impressions of his family. '"And, well, what did you think?" "Oh, best not to say it to your face." Well, thanks a lot!'

The former Archbishop of Canterbury Dr Rowan Williams commented that through numerous meetings with the Sovereign, he had discovered someone with 'real personality': 'I have found in the Queen someone who can be friendly, who can be informal, who can be extremely funny in private – and not everybody appreciates how funny she can be.' Moreover, she is 'quite prepared to tease and to be teased and who, while retaining her dignity always, doesn't stand on her dignity in a conversation'.

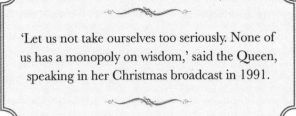

'Let us not take ourselves too seriously. None of us has a monopoly on wisdom,' said the Queen, speaking in her Christmas broadcast in 1991.

Her cousin Margaret Rhodes believes that 'She can uphold the identity of herself as Queen and still be humble. Her inner modesty stops her getting spoiled.'

One of the Queen's closest advisers commented, 'The Queen is the least self-absorbed person you could ever meet. She doesn't tend to talk about herself, and she is not interested in other people's efforts to dwell too much on themselves.'

Daughters-in-Law

The Queen struggled to understand her first daughter-in-law, Princess Diana, who couldn't have been more different in character to Her Majesty. Just two weeks into their marriage, when Charles and Diana came to stay at Balmoral after their honeymoon cruise on board the Royal Yacht *Britannia*, already the cracks in their relationship were showing. Far from the happy, easy-going young girl she had seemed, Diana was moody and withdrawn.

Prince Philip found their stay difficult, saying of the Princess, 'It was just impossible. She didn't appear for breakfast. At lunch she sat with her headphones on, listening to music, and then she would disappear for a walk or run.'

The Queen commented, 'She's like a nervy racehorse. She needs careful handling.'

One of many things in Sarah Ferguson's favour when she became engaged to Prince Andrew as far as the Queen was concerned was that she was down to earth and straightforward. She was an enthusiastic horsewoman who rode regularly with her future mother-in-law and also liked the traditional royal outdoor pursuits of hunting, shooting and fishing. At the time, Sarah said she 'felt favoured and blessed ... I was robust and jolly and not too highly strung.'

The Queen thought Fergie would make an ideal partner for her lively second son, commenting approvingly, 'He's met his match this time!'

When the Queen and Prince Philip did not attend the civil wedding ceremony of Prince Charles and Camilla Parker-Bowles on 9 April 2005 at Windsor Guildhall, there was some press speculation that this reflected the Queen's real feelings about the marriage. In reality, it was a reflection of the Queen's constitutional position and traditional faith rather than a sign of any disapproval. Her genuine happiness at the occasion was apparent in her warm speech later that day. She began by joking that she had an important announcement about the Grand National winner and continued with the racing theme, always close to her heart. She toasted Charles and Camilla saying, 'They have overcome Becher's Brook and The Chair [references to the Grand National's most challenging fences] and all kinds of other obstacles. They have come through and I'm very proud and wish them well. My son is home and dry with the woman he loves. Welcome to the winner's enclosure.'

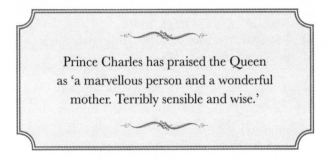

Prince Charles has praised the Queen as 'a marvellous person and a wonderful mother. Terribly sensible and wise.'

Granny Knows Best

Like most matriarchs, the Queen has definite views on her grandchildren's activities. As Sovereign, her opinion carries rather more weight than that of most grandparents.

She is far from impressed by Prince William's love of motorbikes. Explaining his passion, he said, 'It does help being anonymous with my motorcycle helmet on because it does enable me to relax. But I just enjoy everything about motorbikes and the camaraderie that comes with it.'

Prince William apparently spent the evening before his wedding in 2011 riding his motorbike around the late-night London streets. His hobby is said to 'frighten the life out of the Queen' along with other members of the family and their concerns have obviously had an effect. Visiting the Isle of Man TT Race in 2018, the Prince reluctantly admitted, 'I'm a father of three, I have to tone it down.'

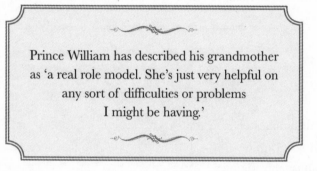

Prince William has described his grandmother as 'a real role model. She's just very helpful on any sort of difficulties or problems I might be having.'

The Queen is also not a fan of Prince Harry's beard. She generally prefers royal men to be clean-shaven, feeling that beards are all very well when away in the Army or out in the wilds but not at home. In fact, so entrenched is the unofficial rule, that the Queen gave her grandson special permission to keep the facial hair when he married Meghan Markle in May 2018. So far, the beard seems set to stay.

Although famously in the public eye, the Royal Family closely guards its private life and in 2009 the Queen stepped in to help Kate Middleton stop private, unofficial photographs of herself being published, by engaging the services of her legal team. The Queen is also quick to recommend personal holidays to her children and grandchildren as far away from the press and public as possible, knowing the importance of time out to maintain healthy relationships.

Royal Birth Traditions

All families cherish their own particular customs, but the Royal Family is in a unique position and has some fairly unusual traditions.

One of the more surprising is that, following a 300-year-old law, the Queen actually has full legal custody of any baby born into the family. The law, called 'The Grand Opinion for the Prerogative Concerning the Royal Family', was introduced by George I in 1717, largely because he did not get along with his son, the future George II, and wanted a greater influence on the upbringing and education of his grandson, the future George III. It has to be said that this is now largely a formality and it is extremely unlikely that the Queen would ever interfere. However, permission is technically needed for children to travel, and Prince Charles and

Diana, for instance, consulted the Queen before taking the young Princes William and Harry on any trips.

The Monarch is the first person to be given the news that a royal baby has been born. It used to be via messenger but it's thought that Prince William told his grandmother of Prince George's birth by phone. Royal births are publicly announced via a notice displayed on an easel outside Buckingham Palace. The typed bulletin is first signed by the attending medical team and includes gender, time of birth, weight and health updates for both mother and baby. No hint as to gender is ever given beforehand. Then it's driven to Buckingham Palace by car and framed, before being displayed at the front of the Palace.

The birth announcement is then followed by a royal 62-gun salute at the Tower of London which lasts some ten minutes. The Union Flag is also raised at the Palace.

It used to be a rule that the Home Secretary had to be present to witness a royal birth, to verify its legitimacy – a real concern in more volatile periods of history. The Queen was quick to dispense with this particular custom when she gave birth to Prince Charles in 1948. In the eighteenth century, it was not unusual for a whole crowd to assemble in the bedchamber to watch the proceedings.

Home Secretaries and sundry others might have been present in the royal delivery room years ago, but not the father. Prince Philip played squash while Prince Charles was being born and it was not until 1964, when general attitudes had changed, that he was there for the birth of his fourth child, Prince Edward, expressly at the invitation of the Queen.

In line with custom, the Queen's royal surgeon-gynaecologist and consultant obstetrician were both present at the births of all three of William and Kate's babies, but Harry and Meghan broke with this tradition, hoping for a home delivery with a female doula and midwife. In the event, though, their son was born at the Portland Hospital in London. The Queen herself opted for home births – when home's a palace and you have command of a full medical team, it must be tempting. Her daughter, Princess Anne, was the first royal to choose a hospital delivery.

In recent years, the new parents usually present their baby to the world just hours after giving birth, appearing on the steps of the Lindo Wing at St Mary's Hospital, Paddington. Following a tradition begun by the Queen with Prince Charles, the newborn is always wrapped in a blanket made by the Nottingham-based company G. H. Hurt & Son. Harry and Meghan also broke with tradition over this. Prince Harry appeared to gathered press and well-wishers a few hours after their baby's birth, but the couple did not present baby Archie until two days later. His birth was also first announced via Instagram.

Typically, names are not revealed for several days. The Queen's opinion is always taken into account, especially for those highest in the order of succession, but nowadays any discussion tends to be an 'informal conversation'. Harry and Meghan have more freedom to choose less traditional names for their children as they are further down the line of succession, and so they defied speculation and took bookmakers completely by surprise when the name Archie Harrison was announced for their firstborn.

Perhaps surprisingly, royal babies do not automatically receive royal titles unless specifically granted by the Sovereign. This follows a Letters Patent granted by George V in 1917 that limited titles within the Royal Family. This means the Queen's great-grandchildren would be Lord or Lady Mountbatten-Windsor rather than HRH or Prince or Princess, apart from the eldest, direct heir to the throne. However, the Queen can issue a new Letters Patent as she did for all William and Kate's future children in 2012. She had previously done so for Prince Andrew's daughters, which is why both Beatrice and Eugenie are Princesses. The Queen had made the same offer to her other two children but Princess Anne refused, preferring her children to have more normal lives, as did Prince Edward and Sophie. According to Debrett's, the eldest son and heir of a duke is allowed to use one of his father's lesser peerage titles as a courtesy. So Harry and Meghan's son could have been the Earl of Dumbarton or Lord Archie had they wished. Thus far they have decided that he will be plain Master Archie Harrison Mountbatten-Windsor with no title and definitely no HRH.

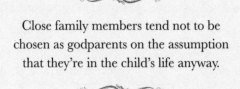

Close family members tend not to be chosen as godparents on the assumption that they're in the child's life anyway.

All royal babies wear the same christening gown, which has been passed down through the generations since the reign of Queen Victoria. The original robe that was made in 1841 for her first child, Princess Victoria, was crafted from Spitalfields silk and Honiton lace, and was worn by 62 royal babies in its 163 years of service. The last to wear it in 2004 was the daughter of Prince Edward and Sophie Wessex, Lady Louise Windsor, at which point it was deemed too fragile to be used again. An exact replica of the gown was duly commissioned and has since been worn by several royal babies, including George, Charlotte and Louis Cambridge.

3

All the Queen's Horses

On 2 June 1953, when you might have expected the young Queen's focus to be on the Coronation ceremony ahead of her, she was instead concerned for her favourite racehorse, Aureole, who was due to run in The Derby four days later. When one of her ladies-in-waiting asked if all was well, the Queen answered cheerfully, 'Oh, yes! The Captain has just rung up to say that Aureole went really well this morning!' In the end the stallion finished second.

Her lifelong love of horses and racing in all its various forms is one she shares with Prince Philip and the rest of the family. As a young woman, she used to ride with her sister and mother.

Jean, Countess of Carnarvon, the wife of the Queen's long-time former racing manager and friend, Henry Porchester, Earl of Carnarvon, remembered the fun the Monarch had choosing names for her foals: 'She would pull on all sorts of knowledge, including old Scottish names.'

The Queen's annual routine is very much in line with that of her horses. She inspects her mares and stallions at the Sandringham stud farm at the start of a new year when the breeding season begins, and then again in April and July when she also looks at the foals from the previous season's mating. Lord Porchester remarked that 'talking to her is almost like talking to a trainer'.

One of the Queen's former trainers, Ian Balding, went further, saying, 'If she had been a normal person, she probably would have become a trainer, she loves it so much.'

In September 1949, the *Daily Telegraph* reported how the young Princess had won her first race with a steeplechaser named Monaveen, whom she co-owned with her mother: 'Princess Elizabeth, who was wearing a beige costume and dark brown hat, was delighted with the result of the race, which she followed closely through binoculars.' Her Majesty is still delighted by the sight of her horses, whether watching them racing or in training on the Downs.

Her former stud manager, Sir Michael Oswald, explained: 'The Queen's diary is drawn up in outline eighteen months in advance, and in detail six months ahead. Only six days are ring-fenced every year and they are the five days of Royal Ascot and Derby Day at Epsom.'

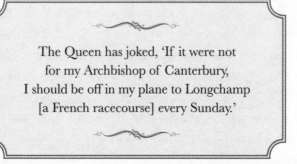

The Queen has joked, 'If it were not for my Archbishop of Canterbury, I should be off in my plane to Longchamp [a French racecourse] every Sunday.'

Her Majesty's sheer enjoyment and excitement at the races is obvious and never more so than when one of her horses is winning. Her joyful exhilaration was caught on film when Free Agent became her twentieth Royal Ascot winner at the Chesham Stakes in 2008. The two-year-old colt broke through almost at the last moment and took the race conclusively. Much to everyone's surprise, the Queen sprang to her feet and punched the air triumphantly shouting, 'I've done it!' Her racing manager John Warren struggled to keep up with the Monarch as she dashed away to greet her horse. 'It was a moment of real joy … she raced to the paddock like she was twenty,' he commented.

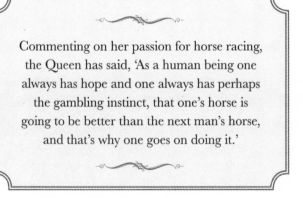

Commenting on her passion for horse racing, the Queen has said, 'As a human being one always has hope and one always has perhaps the gambling instinct, that one's horse is going to be better than the next man's horse, and that's why one goes on doing it.'

Sir Michael Oswald was always impressed by the depth of the Queen's knowledge: 'She reads a lot, and she knows a lot. If you want to discuss a sales catalogue you should do your homework, because she'll know who a horse's great-great-grandmother was.'

Ian Balding remembered how 'she would watch how her horses moved, how they would stretch out. She could see how they run.'

On one memorable occasion, the Queen and Balding were in a field taking a closer look at six young colts that were about to be broken in. Suddenly, the horses went wild, galloping, rearing up and kicking out. Everyone else there dashed for the gate. The only two to remain in place, standing motionless, were the Queen and her trainer who knew that the colts would settle down and would not attack them. When all was again calm, the Queen merely commented, 'Oh, that was scary.'

Balding recalled that the Queen 'was completely unruffled'.

Monty Roberts, a Californian trainer who had also witnessed the Queen's physical courage and came to know her well, believes that 'she has the ability to get calmer in the face of problems rather than allowing herself to get her adrenaline up and to panic'.

The Queen likes to spend time with her horses and knows all the grooms and stable hands personally. Her racing manager and trainers know they can call her at any time on a private line and they enjoy an unrivalled degree of informality with Her Majesty.

John Warren, her current racing manager, says, 'There is no one in the country, perhaps in the industry worldwide, who has bred more crops of foals.' She still has a number of horses in training and keeps around twenty mares that produce fourteen or more foals each season. 'It's rather an intellectual exercise for her to get the breeding right and send the right horse to the right trainer,' Warren explained. 'She has had this incredible unwavering interest. Through good times and bad, the Queen stays steadfast. She never gets down when a foal is born a weakling, and, on the other side, when a Carlton House comes along, she deals with the expectation and, again, remains steadfast.'

When staying away from London, the Queen still rides almost every day and it is clearly something she loves. She famously refuses to wear a hard hat for protection, instead opting for her trademark scarf, leading staff to quip, 'The only thing that comes between the Queen and her heir is a Hermès scarf'. Her stud groom at Windsor Castle explained, 'Here at Windsor, the horses are all about recreation, exercise and fresh air. She rides in all seasons and adores the wild birds, flowers and animals.'

For the Queen, horse riding has always represented freedom, time out and an escape from duty and officialdom, providing space in which to think and be herself. As someone so utterly committed to her job, this is all the more vital for her health and well-being.

Given her interest, it is no surprise that the Queen's first private holiday in the US in 1984 was centred around horses and stud farming. The Queen's West Coast trip and time spent in the Yosemite National Park on a state visit the previous year had piqued her interest in seeing more of the country. It was arranged that she would stay initially at Will and Sarah Farish's ranch in Kentucky – William Stamps Farish III, to give him his full title, is a businessman and former US Ambassador to the UK – and afterwards with Lord Porchester's family at Canyon Ranch in Wyoming.

Following this first stay, the Queen wrote an enthusiastic letter to President Ronald Reagan, describing how she had spent her time in her favourite ways, 'looking at beautiful thoroughbreds' and 'walking in the wide-open spaces by the mountains'.

She was to return to the Kentucky ranch many times. A member of the Queen's staff reflected, 'She felt very much at home in Kentucky. I saw an atmosphere of informality and gaiety that I never saw in England. No one was calling her Ma'am or Your Majesty. She was laughing and joking and having fun. She has a great soft spot for the United States.'

In May 2007, the Queen realized a long-held wish to attend the Kentucky Derby. Along with Prince Philip, she again stayed with Will and Sarah Farish. Relaxing with her old friends, she was also concerned about her granddaughter Zara Phillips's performance at the Badminton Horse Trials that were taking place around the same time, complaining, 'Nobody pays any attention to what Granny thinks!'

The Queen Mother was another avid horse-racing fan, although a patron of National Hunt (jump) racing, while the Queen has always preferred the flat. During their daily phone calls, conversation would invariably turn to horses and all things related. Writing to her mother from New Zealand during the 1953–54 Commonwealth trip, the Queen observed, 'Racing is incredible out here. They all bet like mad and like their marathons of eight races at a dose.'

Prince Philip has always been a keen rider, but less enamoured of horse racing. He has been known to hide a radio in his top hat when attending Royal Ascot in order to listen to the cricket. Generally, he would rather take part than watch: 'I'm not really a talented spectator, frankly … I'd rather *do* something.' In his younger days he played polo, and the thrill of the sport has in turn attracted their sons and grandsons, too. Princes Charles, William and Harry all play, undeterred by the odd knock.

When he felt his polo-playing days were behind him, Prince Philip took up carriage racing, arguably just as risky in terms of injury. He regarded it as the perfect sport for middle age and claimed, rather implausibly given his character, 'I took it up as a geriatric sport. I thought of it as a retirement exercise … I gave up polo when I turned fifty and then this started and I thought, "Well, you've got horses and carriages, why don't you have a go?" So I started in 1973 and it's been going on since then.'

The Prince turned out to have a genuine talent for the sport and although he no longer races competitively, he still drives his own carriage. Waiting for the arrival of Prince Harry and Meghan's first child in May 2019, the 97-year-old

Prince took his horses out for a gallop around Home Park at Windsor, his one concession to age being to take his groom along in the carriage with him.

Princess Anne inherited her mother's love of horses and is also an accomplished horsewoman. She took individual gold in the European Eventing Championship in 1971, and at the same competition four years later she won silver in both the individual and team disciplines.

In 1987, when she was riding in the Dresden Diamond Stakes at Ascot, the Queen shouted encouragement from the stands: 'Don't be so cool – do something!' It obviously did the trick as the Princess went on to win on her horse, Ten No Trumps, becoming the first member of the Royal Family to ride an Ascot winner.

Having represented Britain in the equestrian Three-Day Event at the 1976 Montreal Olympic Games, Princess Anne was very much the proud mother when she presented her daughter, Zara Phillips, with a team silver medal in the Eventing discipline in Greenwich Park during the 2012 London Olympics.

4

Stoic Sovereign

The crown quite literally weighs heavily upon the Queen's head. The Imperial State Crown that is worn by the newly crowned Monarch at the end of the Coronation service is also worn for the annual State Opening of Parliament. Set with some 2,868 diamonds, including the 317-carat Cullinan II diamond, as well as precious stones such as St Edward's Sapphire, The Black Prince's Ruby, and pearls belonging to Elizabeth I, it weighs a whopping 1.06kg.

In a conversation with Alastair Bruce for a programme about her Coronation that aired in January 2018, the Queen revealed just what a physical effort it is to wear the Imperial State Crown at the State Opening of Parliament, during which she is required to read a speech: 'You can't look down to read the speech, you have to take the speech up. Because if you did, your neck would break and it would fall off.'

The crown was made about an inch shorter in height for the Queen than it was when worn by her father, George VI. She explained, 'Fortunately, my father and I have about the same sort of shaped head. But once you put it on, it stays. I mean, it just remains on.'

Although heavy, the Imperial State Crown is considerably lighter than the huge St Edward's Crown, which weighs almost double at 2.23kg. It is the latter that is placed on the

Sovereign's head at the moment of crowning during the Coronation service. Not surprisingly, when wearing it the new Queen had to be helped to climb the platform of five steps to the Chair of Estate, where she sat enthroned ready to receive the Homages of her Peers. Not only did she have to bear the weight of the historic golden crown, but also the ceremonial robes, which weighed nearly 7.7kg, as well as holding the Orb and Sceptre. To move around at all, she relied on the Bishops of Durham, and Bath and Wells.

There was also a point near the beginning of the ceremony when the Queen was completely rooted to the spot. 'I remember one moment when I was going against the pile of the carpet and I couldn't move at all.' The lavishly embroidered robe and carpet were working together, creating friction. 'They hadn't thought of that,' the Sovereign remembered archly. To get going again, the Queen had to ask Archbishop Geoffrey Fisher to give her 'a firm push'!

It takes practice to appear as the serene, unruffled Sovereign. For weeks before her Coronation, Her Majesty went through her lines and every step of the service. She walked around with weighted sheets tied to her shoulders to mimic the heavy robes of state and sat at her desk working with the weighty St Edward's Crown on her head. Even today, after so many years of experience, she will wear the Imperial State Crown for a week or two before the State Opening of Parliament, just to get used to the feel of it again and to ensure she can walk with it set steadily on her head.

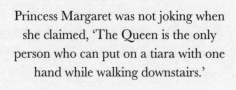

Princess Margaret was not joking when she claimed, 'The Queen is the only person who can put on a tiara with one hand while walking downstairs.'

Striking a Pose

When eminent artist Lucian Freud painted the Queen's portrait in 2000–2001, it took several sittings. During that time, staff grew used to the sight of Her Majesty running late for her mid-morning appointment and hurrying along the Palace corridors dressed in full regalia, complete with ballgown and tiara. Artist and Monarch were said to have got along famously together, discussing racing and horses. Freud's close friend Clarissa Eden said, 'Lucian had a whale of a time with the Queen … She kept on saying, "We must stop talking. We must get on with this portrait."'

When the Queen first sat for a portrait by the well-known American photographer Annie Leibovitz in 2007, she saw a different side to the Queen's personality. Things didn't get off to the best start. The sitting was also being filmed for a television documentary and it had been agreed that the

Queen would wear the Queen Mary's Fringe Tiara, which she had first worn at her wedding, along with her deep-blue velvet Order of the Garter robe and a formal long brocade dress. Time was already tight in the Queen's busy schedule and the normally punctual Monarch arrived late, announcing, 'I don't have much time.'

When the photographer asked the Queen to take off her 'crown' to appear 'less dressy', Her Majesty pointed to the ceremonial robe she was wearing and snapped, 'Less dressy! What do you think this is?'

Leibovitz had spent months preparing and researching settings, looking at previous photographs of the Monarch. She remembered, 'I told the Queen how much I admired Cecil Beaton, and that I was modelling the picture after his, and she said: "You must make your own way, dear." She was mad at me for taking in so much equipment. Apparently, the Queen has this other photographer who only comes with one paper bag of stuff. She likes her so much she helps move the furniture! I love that.'

The Queen did, however, take on board Leibovitz's suggestions and the photographer captured the images she wanted, praising Her Majesty's 'feisty' character and devotion to duty. The Queen was obviously also pleased with the results and Leibovitz was invited back nine years later to take another series of portraits with other members of the family and the dogs for the Queen's 90th birthday in 2016.

The consummate professional, Her Majesty is always aware of camera angles and has an eye for detail. When opening a British Council exhibition of Lucian Freud nudes in Norway, she remarked to an aide that she had been very careful to avoid embarrassing photos, making sure 'I was not photographed between a pair of those great thighs'.

When a curator asked the Queen, 'Haven't you been painted by Lucian Freud, Ma'am?' She laughingly replied, 'Yes, but not like that.'

Good Legs

If asked for the secret of the Queen's apparent strength and energy, her sheer ability to keep going no matter what, most of her advisers will suggest it is down to her naturally healthy constitution, her strong religious faith and the constant support of Prince Philip. Her former Private Secretary Martin Charteris once claimed, 'The Queen is as strong as a yak ... She sleeps well, she's got very good legs and she can stand for a long time.'

The Queen commented upon her own apparent composure under all circumstances: 'I have been trained since childhood never to show emotion in public.'

Ever practical, she also has a trick for standing for hours without getting tired, as she once explained to Susan Crosland, wife of Anthony Crosland, Foreign Secretary in the 1970s: 'One plants one's feet apart like this [whereupon she demonstrated]. Always keep them parallel. Make sure your weight is evenly distributed. That's all there is to it.'

This trick, and the Queen's undoubted stamina, have stood her in good stead. Prime Minister Margaret Thatcher may have been the 'Iron Lady', but she did not possess the Sovereign's physical strength. At a grand reception held annually for diplomats at Buckingham Palace, Mrs Thatcher felt faint among the crowds and in the heat. When the PM was forced to sit down to recover for apparently the second time in Her Majesty's presence, the usually sympathetic Queen glanced across and observed, 'Oh look! She's keeled over again.'

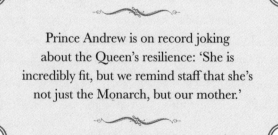

Prince Andrew is on record joking about the Queen's resilience: 'She is incredibly fit, but we remind staff that she's not just the Monarch, but our mother.'

David Airlie, who became the Queen's Lord Chamberlain at the end of 1984, was immediately struck by how 'enormously practical' and 'extremely business-like' she was. He revealed how she attended to matters promptly and generally had the attitude, 'What is the problem? What do we do?' If she delayed, Airlie came to realize it was because she needed time to think. He appreciated how astute she was at judging situations and people. During engagements, for example, 'The reason why she moves slowly is that she wants to absorb what's going on in the room and the people in the room. You can see her looking around the room as she walks in and taking it all in, and my goodness me what she takes in never ceases to amaze me.'

The Queen also has an excellent memory for faces. Meeting a former stable girl who had once looked after her racehorse Highclere, Her Majesty greeted her warmly, knowing immediately who she was. A mere twenty-five years had passed since their last meeting.

The Queen's Smile

The constant pressure on the Queen to smile can be another matter. 'I simply ache with smiling,' she once complained to her Private Secretary Martin Charteris, after reading reports about her grim expression on one of her first state visits. 'The trouble is that women are expected to be smiling all the time. If a man looks solemn it is automatically assumed he is a serious person, concentrating, with grave things on his mind.'

The Queen acknowledged early in her reign that 'unlike my mother, I don't have a naturally smiley face'. In part, this was because the young Princess Elizabeth had taken to heart the advice bestowed by her grandmother Queen Mary that it was inappropriate for a Monarch to smile, and she had 'always assumed people wanted her to look solemn most of the time'.

Portrait painter Michael Noakes was of the opinion that the Monarch 'has no intermediate expression ... a great smile or dour'.

Richard Crossman, the Labour MP and diarist, wrote after a meeting with the young Queen in the 1960s: 'I noticed this time even more than last how shy she can be ... She laughs with her whole face and she cannot just assume a mere smile because she's really a very spontaneous person ... When she is deeply moved and tries to control it, she looks like an angry thundercloud. So very often, when she has been deeply touched by the plaudits of the crowd, she merely looks terribly bad-tempered.'

Former Cabinet Secretary Sir Edward Bridges came to the same conclusion. The Queen was present at a meeting at which Sir Edward was coaching four ministers in ceremonial formalities. Everything went wrong. They were kneeling on the wrong side, then attempted to crawl to their correct positions knocking a book to the floor in the process. The Queen picked it up but looked absolutely furious. Later, Sir Edward returned to apologize. The Queen confessed, 'I nearly laughed.' Sir Edward realized that 'when she looked angry it was mainly because she was trying to stop herself laughing'.

Others have commented that the Queen's smile is genuine rather than a politician's ever-present grin and that she laughs only when she really finds something funny or is moved by the moment.

'She sort of expands when she laughs,' her cousin Margaret Rhodes noted. 'She laughs with her whole face.'

Staff at Sandringham and Balmoral, where the Queen goes to relax and spend time with her family, also reported frequently hearing their Monarch's laughter ringing out.

Tony Parnell, who used to be the foreman at Sandringham, said, 'You can hear her laughter sometimes throughout the house. It is a joyous laugh.'

The Queen's warm humour was often seen in private or when responding to something that Prince Philip shared with her, but it is only in more recent years that she has begun to laugh more openly at public occasions, her gleeful expression often now captured in news photographs.

Howard Morgan, who painted the Queen in the 1980s, was struck by how animated and vivacious the Monarch is away from the public stage. He said, 'Her private side took me totally by surprise. She talks like an Italian. She waves her hands about. She is enormously expressive.'

Ruth Buchanan, the wife of President Dwight D. Eisenhower's Chief of Protocol Wiley T. Buchanan Jr, had very clear memories of the young Queen on her royal tour of North America in 1957: 'She didn't let the barrier down. She would maintain a stance, and she was very much in control of what she did, although she did laugh at my husband's jokes.' Mrs Buchanan went on to say that once, while waiting for her husband to escort the Queen to their car, 'I could hear her guffawing. You didn't realize she had that hearty laugh. But the minute she rounded the corner and saw us, she just straightened up.'

Keep Calm and Carry On

When it comes to the honours system and the bestowing of awards, ceremonies are planned down to the smallest detail. They tend to run like clockwork and the Queen has had plenty of practice. Including OBEs, CBEs and MBEs, around 3,000 medals are presented annually at twenty-two separate ceremonies at Buckingham Palace with more investitures in Edinburgh and Cardiff.

Each medal has a distinct ribbon and leather box and before an investiture ceremony begins, each recipient is told that the Queen will say a few short words to them as she is attaching the insignia to their clothing. The Queen has herself explained: 'One mustn't have a long conversation, obviously, because you'd never finish … but it doesn't always happen.' She recognizes the significance of the awards and by the time of her Diamond Jubilee had personally presided at over 600 investitures. 'People need pats on the back sometimes. It's a very dingy world otherwise,' she believes.

At one ceremony, things got off to a shaky start. Medals had been painstakingly sorted and placed in the right order on a cushion, ready for the Queen to bestow them as people came forward. Unfortunately, moments before the investiture was due to start, a member of staff dropped the cushion and the medals went everywhere.

Without missing a beat, the ever-practical Queen said,

'Just put them any way you can. I'll give them anything and you can sort it out afterwards.' The ceremony went ahead without delay and the Queen calmly carried on as if nothing was wrong. Staff in a side office resolved the muddle and made sure everyone went away with the medal they were due.

Oh, What Fun!

Even with a team of planners organizing royal events and visits, not everything always goes according to plan. But the serene Monarch seems to thrive on the uncertainty. As one lady-in-waiting admitted, 'The Queen rather likes things to go a bit wrong – then she copes.'

After Her Majesty made her review of the Western Fleet from the Royal Barge in Torbay in 1969, the weather grew so stormy that it was decided it would be unsafe to make the step from the Barge back onto the Royal Yacht *Britannia* as usual. Instead, the whole Barge was winched up the side of the Yacht with everyone still inside. Once safely back on *Britannia*'s deck the Queen was matter-of-fact. 'Well, that was fun, wasn't it?'

In summer 1977, Silver Jubilee fever gripped the country with the Queen's official birthday marking the start of the festivities. On the evening of 6 June, the Queen stood on Snow Hill in Windsor Great Park, poised to light the beacon that was to be the sign for a series of others to be lit right across the country, just as they had been in the days of the Spanish Armada. Pageant master and pyrotechnics expert Major Sir Michael Parker had worried that the huge beacon would not light fast enough, so he had packed it with fireworks and stationed a Royal Signals Major next to a detonator, just in case.

Before the Queen had a chance to light the beacon herself, the soldier, poised and trigger-happy, pressed the detonator. The bonfire blazed into flames and the Monarch stepped back and laughed, 'I can't think why you bothered to ask me.'

There were then problems with the sound system and a deafening firework mortar set off instead of a flare. 'Your Majesty, I'm afraid it's all going terribly wrong,' confessed Sir Michael. 'In fact, everything that could possibly go wrong is going wrong.'

'Oh good!' the Queen replied, beaming. 'What fun!'

In the Face of Danger

The Queen's stoicism goes way beyond physical stamina and an admirable ability to keep her head when chaos reigns around her.

While Her Majesty was on a visit to Northern Ireland in 1966, a young republican threw a 4 kg concrete block at the royal car as it drove slowly past. He was aiming for the glass sunroof, but instead hit the car's bonnet. Quickly recovering her composure after the initial shock, the Queen said simply, 'It's a strong car.'

Celebrating her official birthday on 13 June 1981, the Queen led the traditional Trooping the Colour parade as it set off from Buckingham Palace along the Mall towards Horse Guards Parade. She was riding her favoured horse, Burmese – the black mare given to her by the Royal Canadian Mounted Police in 1969 – for the thirteenth time during the birthday procession. Just before eleven o'clock, six shots were fired at the Queen from the crowd. Startled, Burmese bolted forward almost unseating Her Majesty. The unflappable Queen pulled on the reins, entirely focused on calming and settling her horse. She continued at a walking pace, smiling at the crowd, completing the ceremony. The bullets turned out to be blanks, fired by seventeen-year-old Marcus Sarjeant. He was quickly tackled and arrested by a collection of guards-men, onlookers and police, and later sentenced to five years in prison after being convicted under the 1842 Treason Act for 'wilfully discharging at the person of Her Majesty the Queen a blank cartridge pistol with intent to alarm her'.

The Queen admitted afterwards that in the instant before the shots rang out she had actually glimpsed the gunman aiming at her from the crowd, but couldn't quite believe what she was seeing. She also said of Burmese, 'It wasn't the shots that frightened her – but the Cavalry!' On hearing the shots, two Cavalrymen had spurred their horses forwards to ride by the Queen's side, which had further unsettled her horse.

Not surprisingly, after the incident security was reviewed and it was agreed that in future members of the Household Cavalry would flank the Monarch as protection during the parade. When one of the first took his place beside her the following year, the Queen joked, 'You know why you're here. You're the one to get shot, not me.'

Press and public were united in admiration of the Queen's resilience. The *Daily Express* summed it up: 'Her Majesty showed guts, courage, pluck, bravery and bottle.'

The following year, the Queen woke in the early hours of a July morning to find a strange man standing by her bed. He was Michael Fagan, barefoot and bleeding from where he'd cut his hand breaking in through a Buckingham Palace window. With impressive cool, the Queen chatted calmly before she managed to alert security, using the excuse of fetching Fagan a cigarette to get away. When the police finally arrived, one stopped to straighten his tie upon seeing Her Majesty. 'Oh, come on!' chivvied the exasperated Queen. 'Get a bloody move on.'

Her footman Paul Whybrew commented that he thought it was Michael Fagan rather than the Queen who looked in need of a stiff drink to calm his nerves.

Later, the Queen amused family and friends with the story, including a chambermaid's startled reaction – 'Bloody 'ell Ma'am, what's 'e doin' 'ere?' – with a perfect impersonation of the girl's Yorkshire accent.

The tightened security measures at all the royal palaces that followed the break-in also caused a problem for the Queen. Unable to sleep one night, the Monarch decided to take a stroll in Buckingham Palace's gardens, her preferred remedy for insomnia. A zealous security guard saw someone moving in the shadows. 'Who's there?' he challenged, when a familiar figure stepped out into the light.

'Bloody hell, Your Majesty!' exclaimed the surprised guard. 'I nearly shot you.' He swiftly apologized for his language.

The Queen was unruffled by the language or loaded gun, quipping, 'That's quite all right. Next time I'll ring through beforehand, so you don't have to shoot me.'

The Queen generally takes a robust approach to threats to her life, adopting a fatalistic attitude and acknowledging, 'If someone wants to get me, it is too easy.'

In 1961, she was invited to Ghana as a guest of President Kwame Nkrumah who had led his country to independence in 1957. Prime Minister Harold Macmillan did not want the Sovereign to accept as there was a very real threat to the President's life at the time and there were fears that the Queen might be in danger if there was an assassination attempt during her stay. The visit had been agreed two years before and Her Majesty insisted on going. Determined not to bow to pressure from 'faint hearts in Parliament and the press', she told the Prime Minister in no uncertain terms that she 'meant to be a Queen and not a puppet', adding, 'How silly I should look if I was scared to visit Ghana and then Khrushchev [the Soviet Premier] went and had a good reception.'

Despite a spate of bombings in the capital Accra, the Queen joined President Nkrumah as they drove through packed streets in an open-top Rolls-Royce. She charmed both the President and the local press who called her, 'The greatest Socialist Monarch in the world.' A BBC news reporter commented, 'In that open car ... she didn't bat an eyelid – Nkrumah next to her. You just saw the Queen very calm, very poised – not smiling too much – just right.'

In 1979, advisers warned the Queen against visiting Zambia as part of her proposed tour of Africa. At the time, the country was involved in the long colonial war with its neighbour Southern Rhodesia which was trying to establish itself as independent Zimbabwe. Officials felt the visit would bring the royal party perilously close to the war zone. The Queen was not to be deterred and on 28 July enthusiastic crowds in Lusaka, the Zambian capital, greeted the Queen, Prince Philip and Prince Andrew. The Queen is said to have told her security advisers, 'Of course I'm going. You can see that I don't get shot.'

The Queen was slightly more concerned about safety on the Royal Yacht *Britannia* during a state visit to France in 1992 when it was anchored at Bordeaux. Following the on-board state banquet for President François Mitterrand, several hundred extra guests had been invited onto the Yacht to watch a traditional performance by the Band of the Royal Marines on the quayside. *Britannia*'s crew ensured the visitors were evenly spread along the deck, while the duty officer carefully monitored the Yacht's angle of tilt. With everyone watching from one side, the barges were lowered over the other to counterbalance the extra weight. What no one was aware of was that the French President had arranged a surprise firework display to begin the moment the Band finished playing. As the first rockets took off, all the guests surged to the opposite, already weighted, side. *Britannia* lurched dangerously.

Britannia's Commander Sir Robert Woodard remembered, 'The whole Yacht went right over, to the point that the Queen asked me: "Are we going to be all right?" ... I said, "Of course, we are." Because there was no point in both of us panicking.'

Through It All

Throughout her life, the Queen has been sustained by a strong personal faith. During her Coronation, one of the most important parts of the ceremony was the anointing. The film cameras were turned off in Westminster Abbey as the young Queen, dressed in a simple white linen robe, was seated on King Edward's Chair under a silk canopy. Geoffrey Fisher, the Archbishop of Canterbury, poured holy oil into a twelfth-century anointing spoon, making the sign of the cross on her forehead, palms of her hands and chest, as he anointed Queen Elizabeth II.

Canon John Andrew, a friend of the Royal Family as well as senior chaplain to the next Archbishop of Canterbury, Michael Ramsey, explained, 'The real significance of the Coronation for her was the anointing, not the crowning. She was consecrated and that makes her Queen. It is the most solemn thing that has ever happened in her life. She cannot abdicate. She is there until death.'

Former Archbishop of Canterbury George Carey has also emphasized the 'sacramental manner in which she views her own office', seeing her faith as part of her duty, 'not in the sense of a burden, but of glad service'. He believes this is what strengthens the Queen and enables her to deal with even the most difficult problems: 'She has a comfortable relationship with God. She's got a capacity because of her faith to take anything the world throws at her. Her faith comes from a theology of life that everything is ordered.'

Her Majesty worships every Sunday wherever she is in the world. Lord Carey has commented that the Queen 'treasures Anglicanism. She loves the 1662 Book of Common Prayer, which is always used at Sandringham. She would disapprove of modern services, but wouldn't make that view known. The Bible she prefers is the old King James version. She has a great love of the English language and enjoys the beauty of the words. The scriptures are soaked into her.'

As with many of the large country estates in Britain, the preachers at Balmoral or Sandringham church services are usually visiting ministers, and the Queen and Prince Philip will often invite them to stay. As a result, members of the clergy see a more relaxed side of the Royal Family. 'They say what they think in front of us,' remarked a Church of Scotland minister.

Lord Carey has reflected on the difference between the Queen and Prince Philip's attitudes to faith: 'His approach is much more restless than the Queen, more focused on the intellectual side.'

Speaking in 2011, the Archbishop of York John Sentamu said of Prince Philip: 'Bishops who are invited to stay and preach at Sandringham face a barrage of serious theological questions over lunch, and there is nowhere to hide … In my case, the sermon was based on Jesus turning water into wine at Cana of Galilee. The Duke suggested many possible explanations for the miracle, including a Uri Geller-type explanation, and he produced a spoon which Uri Geller had bent for him. To my rescue came that still small voice of calm from Her Majesty the Queen, saying, "Philip and his theories ..."'

Troubled Times

With typical understatement, the Queen remarked of one of the worst years of her reign that 1992 'is not a year on which I shall look back with undiluted pleasure. In the words of one of my more sympathetic correspondents, it has turned out to be an "*Annus Horribilis*".'

The year had begun badly in January with the publication of compromising photographs of Sarah, Duchess of York, on holiday with oil tycoon Steve Wyatt. Shortly after came press pictures of Princess Diana, sad and alone, at the Taj Mahal, the famed monument to love and marriage. In March, the Duke and Duchess of York announced they were to formally separate and in April, Princess Anne and Captain Mark Phillips went a step further and divorced on the grounds of his adultery. Princess Anne went on to quietly remarry Commander Tim Laurence in December.

The summer brought further scandal for the Royal Family as Andrew Morton's tell-all book about Princess Diana was published, documenting in stark detail her struggles with bulimia and depression inside a loveless marriage. Then came the infamous toe-sucking photographs of the Duchess of York, this time with her financial adviser, John Bryan. By this point it seemed to be open season on the royals and nothing was off limits. Embarrassment continued when *The Sun* printed the transcript of the so-called 'Squidgygate' tapes of an intimate phone call between Princess Diana and James Gilbey. The Palace declined to comment.

Any hopes the year might at least end quietly were dashed on 20 November, when a serious fire broke out at Windsor Castle, the place that the Queen had always considered home. Photographs showed the Monarch standing alone in the courtyard, huddled in a raincoat against the rain, watching the devastation as the fire continued to blaze. Her expression said it all. December saw the announcement that Charles and Diana were to formally separate and, in a final blow, the transcript of the Queen's Christmas speech was leaked to the press.

The Queen made her *Annus Horribilis* comment at the start of a speech she gave at the Guildhall in London, just four days after the Windsor fire. She was guest of honour at a lunch to celebrate the 40th anniversary of her accession to the throne. The Queen was suffering from a heavy cold and sore throat, and had a temperature of 101°C, probably as a result of standing outside in the cold and rain, watching her beloved home burn.

The Queen's speech continued: 'I sometimes wonder how future generations will judge the events of this tumultuous year. I dare say that history will take a slightly more moderate view than that of some contemporary commentators … [Distance can] lend an extra dimension to judgement, giving it a leavening of moderation and compassion – even of wisdom – that is sometimes lacking in the reactions of those whose task it is in life to offer instant opinions on all things great and small … No institution … should expect to be free from the scrutiny of those who give it their loyalty and support, not to mention those who don't … But … that scrutiny … can be just as effective if it is made with a touch of gentleness, good humour and understanding. This sort of questioning can also act, and it should do so, as an effective engine for change.'

Modernizing Monarch

A lesser character might have been tempted to give up or wallow in self-pity, but that is not in the Queen's nature. In her Christmas speech that year, the Monarch focused on the example of Group Captain Leonard Cheshire. His bravery during the Second World War had earned him a Victoria Cross and his tireless work since on behalf of the disabled had been rewarded by an Order of Merit. The Queen had met the former RAF pilot again earlier in the year, shortly before his death from a long illness. She said the meeting 'did as much as anything in 1992 to help me put my own worries into perspective ... He made no reference to his own illness, but only to his hopes and plans to make life better for others.' The Queen ended by pledging to meet the new challenges of the coming year 'with fresh hope' and reaffirmed her 'commitment to your service'.

Following on from the year of scandal and revelation, the Queen took on board the criticisms she had received. Both she and Prince Charles announced they would pay taxes on their private incomes and allow greater financial scrutiny by parliament. It was announced that Buckingham Palace would open to the paying public to raise funds for the repairs to Windsor Castle. The civil list was reduced and the Queen agreed to meet the bulk of the family's expenses from her own Duchy of Lancaster income.

The Queen realized that the monarchy needed to adapt and evolve, using public relations and introducing market research. The 'Way Ahead Group' was formed in the mid-1990s, bringing together senior family members and advisers in twice-yearly meetings. Among many other changes it was this group that brought about the Succession to the Crown Act in 2013, removing male preference. 'We were future-proofing,' said a member of the Royal Household, referring to the reforms that were made.

Constitutional expert Professor Vernon Bogdanor credits the Queen with overseeing major changes in her reign, transforming from 'a rather magical monarchy to a public service monarchy'. Television, and more lately social media, changed the Crown's relationship with the public for ever and has resulted in far less privacy. Bogdanor has also commented that 'in nineteen fifty-two we were a very deferential society. Apparently, one-third of people thought she had been chosen by God.' He explained that previously the monarchy was 'distant and remote ... [now] it is a much more utilitarian institution to be judged by what it contributes to public service and community feeling'.

Royal Tragedy

Nothing could have prepared the Queen or the Royal Family for the shocking death of Diana, Princess of Wales in a Paris car crash in the early hours of 31 August 1997. It was a huge blow for the family and a tragic loss for her young sons. The outpouring of public grief for the adored Princess was overwhelming. Nothing like it had been seen before in Britain and at first the Queen had absolutely no idea how to respond.

As always at that time of year, the Queen and Prince Philip were staying at Balmoral along with William and Harry when they heard the terrible news. Their first instinct was to look after their grandsons and do everything they could to protect them. They remained in Scotland away from the glare of publicity to care for the young Princes. This led many to criticize their approach and accuse the Sovereign of being out of touch with the prevailing mood of the country. It was a dangerous moment for the monarchy.

Anger focused on the failure of Buckingham Palace to fly the Union Flag as a mark of respect to the Princess. It was long-established royal protocol that only the Royal Standard was ever flown above the Palace and then only when the Monarch was in residence. Downing Street Director of Communications Alastair Campbell, who was always acutely aware of the mood of the media, telephoned the Palace to warn them: 'I don't know what those journalists are up to, but it's something to do with the flagpole.'

Finally, the Queen asked that the Union Flag should fly at half-mast above the Palace and a new tradition was established. From that time the Union Flag is generally raised whenever the Queen is away and is lowered to half-mast at times of national and international mourning.

There was also no question of there being a private family funeral. Instead, a royal ceremonial service was planned at Westminster Abbey with full pageantry and the funeral cortège processing through the streets from St James's Palace.

When the Queen, Prince Philip and the two Princes left Scotland to fly back for Diana's funeral, there was a sense that the public mood was shifting and the atmosphere was thawing. Staff watching the family arrive at Buckingham Palace remembered: 'As the Queen came down in a car you could hear the crowd beginning to clap, and it was a bit ragged at first, and then it became warmer.'

Later, the Queen and Prince Philip went outside to meet the gathered crowds and look at the sea of flowers banked high against the Palace railings and carpeting the Mall. You could almost feel the animosity lifting. When the Queen walked through Kensington Palace Gardens where the floral tributes lay everywhere, a girl stepped forward with a small bunch of flowers. 'Are these for Diana?' the Queen asked. 'No, Ma'am, for you.' Her Majesty was noticeably moved.

On the eve of Diana's funeral the Queen broadcast a speech explaining her position in a way she had never really done before. 'What I say to you now, as your Queen and a grandmother, I say from my heart.' She paid tribute to Diana and went on to say that by staying at Balmoral, 'We have all been trying to help William and Harry come to terms with the devastating loss that they and the rest of us have suffered.' Her Majesty finished with a hope for the future, saying that 'I for one believe that there are lessons to be drawn from her life and from the extraordinary and moving reaction to her death,' and that the Princess's funeral was a time 'to show the whole world the British nation united in grief and respect'.

The tragedy changed perceptions for ever and accelerated

the pace of change for the Royal Household. After Diana's death, priorities were reassessed. There was a general change of tone and the realization that new ways of doing things had to be found.

When interviewed by Andrew Marr, journalist and biographer of the Queen Robert Lacey summed things up: 'I think the reign of Elizabeth II will be looked back on above all in terms not of the particular political crises, but of the way in which the monarchy adapted to the media, was nearly brought crashing down by the media – I'm thinking of what happened at the time of Diana's death – and has since emerged into calmer waters.'

Jubilee Celebrations

Five years later, the Queen saw her Golden Jubilee celebrations as an opportunity to thank people for their support. She is reputed to have said, 'I have to be seen to be believed' and she did her best to put that into practice during 2002. She and Prince Philip circumnavigated the globe, starting with visits to Jamaica, New Zealand and Australia, taking in seventy cities and towns throughout the UK over thirty-eight days. Throughout the year, they clocked up over 40,000 miles.

The Golden Jubilee was celebrated across the world in myriad ways: a party was held by scientists of the British

Antarctic Survey in temperatures of minus 20°C; the Empire State Building in New York shone purple and gold for the occasion; 2,006 beacons were lit on 3 June, stretching from the Arctic to the Antarctic, creating the largest chain ever.

Buckingham Palace's gardens were used for public concerts for the first time and a CD of the 'Party at the Palace' concert sold 100,000 copies in its first week. The Queen was the first member of the Royal Family to be presented with a gold disc by the record industry.

In 2012, the Queen became only the second monarch in British history to celebrate her Diamond Jubilee, following on from Queen Victoria in 1897. If 1992 marked a nadir for the crown, 2012 proved a highlight, rewarding the Queen for her hard work, dedication and stoicism. It was apparent from the cheering, flag-waving crowds that the monarchy had never been more popular.

This time, as a nod to her eighty-six years, the Queen and Prince Philip travelled around Britain, but left the overseas trips to other members of the Royal Family. The Jubilee weekend in June saw a Thames Pageant with a flotilla of 1,000 boats sailing along the river and a concert in front of Buckingham Palace. A network of over 4,200 beacons were lit and the Queen attended a National Service of Thanksgiving at St Paul's Cathedral. It was also during her Diamond Jubilee year that the Queen opened both the London 2012 Olympic Games and Paralympic Games, as well as initiating various environmental and cultural projects.

The Sapphire Queen

On 6 February 2017, the Queen celebrated another royal milestone quietly at Sandringham. The date marked the 65th anniversary of her accession to the throne. The day before, the smiling Monarch was filmed greeting waiting well-wishers after the Sunday morning service at St Mary Magdalene church.

It is tempting to wonder what the young Princess Elizabeth would have thought, had she been told at the age of twenty-five when she first became Queen, that she would go on to become the first British monarch to celebrate their Sapphire Jubilee. Almost eighteen months earlier, on 9 September 2015, Queen Elizabeth II had become Britain's longest-serving sovereign, though she commented that breaking the record held by her great-great-grandmother Queen Victoria was 'not one to which I have ever aspired'. In British history, there are only five other monarchs who have reigned for more than half a century: Victoria was on the throne for over 63 years, George III for 59 years, James VI of Scotland (also known as James I of England) for more than 57 years, Henry III for 56 years and Edward III for 50 years.

Now into her tenth decade, as the stoical Sovereign begins to step back, just a little, and the younger generation of royals take on more public duties, it is clear that the monarchy has embraced change, emerging stronger than ever.

Looking back, Her Majesty has reflected, 'Inevitably, a long life can pass by many milestones. My own is no exception.'

5

A Question of Diplomacy

The model of diplomacy, remaining famously tight-lipped in public on her real opinions, the Queen has often been called upon to soothe tensions in matters of state. Over the years, Her Majesty has become very used to meeting all sorts of different people from every walk of life, treating all with equal courtesy. She has always tried to put them at ease and ask relevant questions, but even the Queen was at a loss for words when a guest at one of the Buckingham Palace garden parties asked the Monarch, 'What is it you do?' Talking about it later, the Queen admitted that she had absolutely no idea how to answer.

State Visits and Visitors

Even ardent republicans are not immune to her charms. In the early 1980s, Australian Labor [*sic*] leader Bob Hawke predicted, 'The Queen is a decent hard-working lady doing a useful job but, by the end of the century, the monarchy will be phased out.' In fact, the results of the 1999 Australian republic referendum would decide otherwise. But when the sceptical politician actually met the Queen during her Commonwealth visit in 1986, when he was Prime Minister, he was won over, enthusing, 'She has arguably got the most difficult job in the world, and she discharges it with an absolutely remarkable capacity and composure, relieved by a magnificent sense of humour.'

When eggs were thrown at the Queen's car in New Zealand during the same 1986 tour, one of them cracked on her pink coat. Her Majesty was unsurprisingly alarmed at first, but quickly regained her composure to joke that she generally preferred her eggs 'for breakfast'.

Queen in Waiting

The state visit to Morocco in October 1980 proved somewhat chaotic and there are several photographs showing the Queen waiting for her host King Hassan II to arrive. As the temperature rose in the already hot and airless tea tent, the usually patient Queen quipped to photographers, 'Keep your cameras trained; you may see the biggest walkout of all time.'

As part of the Diamond Jubilee celebrations in 2012, the Queen invited monarchs from around the world to a lunch at Windsor Castle. As far as Her Majesty is concerned, unless you abdicate you remain a king or queen even if you have been deposed and your country is now staunchly republican. Devising a seating plan for the official photograph, however, was a nightmare for protocol – how do you rank a roomful of royals without offending an emperor or king? The Queen came up with the perfect solution. As the host, she would sit in the middle with all the other monarchs positioned according to the date of their accession. The Kings of Romania and Bulgaria ended up on either side of her, though neither remained on their country's throne.

The model of diplomacy in most situations, the straight-talking Monarch understands how to cut to the chase and is also known not to pull any punches when necessary. On one notable occasion, an ambassador was tying himself in knots trying to use various polite euphemisms and complicated psychiatric terms to describe a particularly erratic politician. The Queen listened for a while and then said, 'What you are really saying is that he is bonkers.'

In 1984, there was an unlikely hitch when the Monarch landed at Lexington in Kentucky. The Queen is not required to carry a passport – they are issued on her authority and in her name after all – but an over-zealous US customs official was determined to stick to the rules and would not allow Her Majesty to enter the USA as she had neither passport nor visa to prove her identity, though it was absolutely obvious who she was. A phone call to Washington, D.C. swiftly solved the problem.

Staff at Buckingham Palace agreed they had seldom seen the Queen as furious as she was in 1973 upon finding out that the wife of one of the Commonwealth leaders had smuggled a dog not only into the country, but also inside the Palace.

US Presidents

She was Her Royal Highness Princess Elizabeth when she first met Dwight D. 'Ike' Eisenhower during the Second World War while he was in London as Supreme Allied Commander.

The Queen's cousin, Margaret Rhodes, wrote about an unlikely incident involving George VI and General Eisenhower that happened during her wartime stay at Windsor Castle. It was a sunny summer afternoon. The King and Queen, Princesses Elizabeth and Margaret, together with Margaret Rhodes were all having tea on a terrace overlooking the Castle's rose garden. The table was formally set with a long white tablecloth and silver kettle. Part-way through they heard voices. The King exclaimed, 'Oh Lord, General Eisenhower and his group are being shown round the Castle. I quite forgot. We will all be in full view when they turn the next corner.' The terrace was positioned in such a way that the royal party would have been clearly seen, but unable to come down or speak to the visitors. 'Without another word, and acting as one, the Royal Family dived under the tablecloth,' Margaret Rhodes recalled. If the General and his group had glanced up at the terrace, they would have seen 'a table shaking from the effect of the concerted and uncontrollable giggles of those sheltering beneath it'.

Years later, in 1957, when the Queen met President Eisenhower again on her first royal visit to the US as

Sovereign, she told him the story of the wartime tea party, which he found very funny. During the American trip, enthusiastic crowds turned out to see the Queen and Prince Philip wherever they went and at one point a congressman shouted out, 'We have all fallen in love with the Queen, Ike!'

The Royal Couple had quite a tour around the East Coast, including a visit to Jamestown, Virginia, which had been the first British settlement in the New World in the seventeenth century, as well as to Washington, D.C. and New York City. As part of their trip, the Queen had asked to see an American football game and she sat in a specially constructed 'royal box' on the 50-yard line to watch the University of Maryland play the University of North Carolina. To the cheers of 43,000 fans, the 'little British Sovereign' as she was called, walked on to the field to talk to a player from both teams.

Following on from the football game, the royal party were taken to a supermarket. It's hard to imagine what a novelty this was, but at the time supermarkets were rare phenomena in Britain and neither the Queen nor Prince Philip had ever been inside one before. They were surprised by the sheer range and quantities of goods on offer in contrast to Great Britain where post-war austerity was still very much in evidence. Shopping trollies were also something new. 'How nice that you can bring your children along,' the Queen said, pointing to the little bench seat in one.

The Queen's final request was for a visit to Manhattan,

somewhere she had wanted to see since childhood, but 'as it should be approached' from the water. At her first sight of the famous downtown skyline, from the deck of a US army ferry, the Queen was like any other excited tourist. 'Wheee!' she exclaimed, before likening the outline to 'a row of great jewels'.

During the trip, the Queen also met with former President Herbert Hoover, as well as future President Richard Nixon, who was then Vice President.

The American and British press pronounced the visit a huge success and in a letter to the Royal Couple, Eisenhower wrote, 'You both have captivated the people of our country by your charm and graciousness.'

In June 1959, the Queen and Prince Philip undertook a six-week tour of Canada, stopping in every territory and province. They also took time out to entertain the Eisenhowers at lunch on board the Royal Yacht *Britannia* and briefly visited Chicago. The Mayor there declared, 'Chicago is yours!' President Eisenhower had provided an official limousine for the Royal Couple and afterwards wrote that his chauffeur claimed he had 'never witnessed greater enthusiasm among the crowds lining the streets'.

The Queen had an affectionate relationship with the former General and he often saw the more relaxed and homely side of the Monarch. Stopping off in Britain as part of his world tour in late August 1959, President Eisenhower, his wife Mamie and son John flew to Aberdeen where Prince

Philip was waiting to take them to Balmoral to stay with the Royal Family and guests. When the rest of the party went off to the grouse moor for a day's shooting, the President didn't join them, staying behind with the Queen who was then pregnant with Prince Andrew. They shared a picnic and the Queen made him drop scones on a griddle. She had learned how to bake and make cakes from a cook at Windsor Castle during the war. The President thought the scones were delicious and was so impressed he asked for the recipe. The Queen would later write it out for him, in a letter penned the following January, including the instruction that 'the mixture needs a great deal of beating'.

When Eisenhower left to meet with Prime Minister Harold Macmillan at Chequers he called his stay at Balmoral 'perfect in every respect'.

In June 1961, the Queen and Prince Philip entertained President John F. Kennedy and his wife Jackie at a lavish state banquet at Buckingham Palace. It was the first time a US President had dined there since the end of the First World War, when the Queen's grandfather George V had entertained President Woodrow Wilson.

The First Lady confessed to the Queen that she found official tours very pressured and tiring. The Monarch was sympathetic, confiding, 'One gets crafty after a while and learns how to save oneself.'

Afterwards, Jackie Kennedy was less than diplomatic, telling Gore Vidal that she had found the Queen 'pretty heavy going' and that she suspected 'the Queen resented me. Philip was nice, but nervous. One felt absolutely no relationship between them.' It's likely the Queen heard at least some of the comments, especially as the First Lady had also criticized the furnishings, flowers and the Queen's personal style to royal photographer Cecil Beaton.

Ever diplomatic, the gossip did not stop the Queen from entertaining Jackie Kennedy and her sister Lee Radziwill a few months later at a lunch at Buckingham Palace. This time, the two seemed to get along well and afterwards, the Queen wrote to President Kennedy, saying, 'It was a great pleasure to meet Mrs Kennedy again.' For her part, the President's wife was notably discreet when asked by the press about her lunch: 'I don't think I should say anything about it except how grateful I am and how charming she was.'

The Queen was not to meet JFK again. On 22 November 1963 came the shocking news of his assassination and the Queen united with the rest of the world in sorrow at the event. 'The unprecedented intensity of that wave of grief mixed with something akin to disaster that swept over our people at the news of President Kennedy's assassination was a measure of the extent to which we recognized what he had already accomplished and of the high hopes that rode with him in a future that was not to be.'

Prince Philip and Prime Minister Alec Douglas-Home flew to Washington, D.C. for the funeral, but as the Queen was pregnant with Prince Edward at the time she was advised by her doctors not to fly. They also warned against attending the memorial service at St Paul's Cathedral. Instead, she held her own service at St George's Chapel at Windsor, inviting American servicemen stationed in the UK.

In May 1965, the Queen dedicated a memorial to the President at Runnymede, the site where the Magna Carta was sealed in 1215. Jackie Kennedy and her children walked with the Queen and Prince Philip to the ceremony, the Kennedys' young son John holding the Prince's hand. The Queen spoke simply, from the heart, paying tribute to JFK's 'wit and style', mentioning the President's ties to Britain and ending, 'With all our hearts, my people shared his triumphs, grieved at his reverses and wept at his death.' The Kennedy Memorial Trust, established by the British government, awards scholarships for British postgraduate students to study at Harvard University or Massachusetts Institute of Technology (MIT).

Moving swiftly past President Jimmy Carter, who committed the ultimate faux pas by kissing the Queen Mother on the lips when visiting Buckingham Palace to attend a NATO event in May 1977 … He was apparently trying to favourably compare her to his own cherished mother, but completely misjudged the situation. Afterwards, the Queen Mother said, 'I took a sharp step backwards, not quite far enough.' This was the second, and final, time that President Carter met the Queen. Special relations of a more formal kind were re-established with his presidential successor.

The 'Special' Relationship

During Queen Elizabeth II's long reign there have been thirteen different US Presidents so far, beginning with Harry S. Truman. She has met with all but one on state visits in Britain and America (she missed meeting Lyndon B. Johnson). It would be fair to say that some relations have been more special than others.

President Ronald Reagan was the first US President to stay overnight at Windsor Castle along with his wife Nancy, in June 1982. Writing in his memoir, he described it as a 'fairy-tale visit' and said that staying there was one of his favourite experiences as President.

The Queen and the President shared a passion for horse riding and enjoyed riding together in Windsor's Home Park. Photographs taken at the time show how at ease the two were in each other's company. Reagan commented that the Queen was 'charming ... and down-to-earth', and when she was riding Burmese, her black mare, he observed that 'she was in charge of that animal!'

When the Queen landed in California during her 1983 US tour, she had expected sunshine. Instead, it was pouring with rain, prompting the Queen's dry sense of humour to come to the fore. 'I knew before we came that we had exported many of our traditions to the United States. I had not realized before that the weather was one of them.'

The unusual weather caused a few wardrobe malfunctions for the normally well-prepared Monarch. When making state visits, the Queen has to have clothes for every eventuality, which effectively means a choice of at least three outfits a day plus a set of mourning clothes, 'just in case'. Her travel staff make sure the royal luggage arrives safely ahead of Her Majesty. However, everyone had expected West Coast sunshine and the Queen had an array of light dresses to match the weather. When met by the worst storms there for decades, the Queen had no option but to keep wearing the same serviceable raincoat. It appeared in every photo until Princess Margaret was driven to suggest that her sister should really consider buying another coat.

Arriving at the Reagans' Rancho del Cielo near Santa Barbara in another torrential downpour, following a tortuous jeep ride, the Queen's habitual good humour and ability to make the best of anything was apparent. 'It's an adventure!' she exclaimed, enthusiastically.

The Queen had a long-cherished desire to see the West Coast of the USA, and had been disappointed when it was cut from her 1957 tour 'for reasons of time and protocol'. Now she and Prince Philip were there at the personal invitation of the Reagans and the timing seemed ideal. As the Queen commented, 'What better time than when the President is a Californian?'

The Queen and President Reagan developed a friendship over the years which went beyond the polite formalities of two heads of state. After her visit in 1983, the Reagans were again in the UK in 1984 and 1988.

In 1989, the Queen granted Reagan an honorary knighthood, the highest distinction that someone who is not British can receive. It was in recognition of the President's help to the UK during the Falklands War in 1982, and she presented him with the honorary Knight Grand Cross of the Most Honourable Order of the Bath after a formal lunch at Buckingham Palace. This made the by then former US President, Sir President Ronald Reagan. He said on record how incredibly proud he was to receive such an honour.

When it came to the official speeches during a royal state visit in 1991, President George Bush Senior failed to lower the height of the lectern and microphone for the Queen, meaning that all most of the audience could see was the top of her purple-striped hat.

'All I got is a talking hat!' an NBC commentator said.

The Queen saw the funny side of this and, a few days later, when she became the first British Monarch to address Congress, she began her speech by joking, 'I do hope you can see me today.'

Former British diplomat and Ambassador to the US Sir David Manning said of the Queen's relationship with President Bush Senior, 'She was very comfortable with Bush [President number] forty-one. It was a very warm relationship.' He went on to add, 'She had an easy rapport with Bush forty-three, too.'

As part of celebrations to mark the 50th anniversary of D-Day in 1994, the Queen and Prince Philip hosted a banquet in Portsmouth and invited US President Bill Clinton and his wife Hillary to stay overnight on board

Britannia. After spending time talking to the Monarch, President Clinton was struck by 'the clever manner in which she discussed public issues, probing me for information and insights without venturing too far into expressing her own political views … Her Majesty impressed me as someone who, but for the circumstances of her birth, might have become a successful politician or diplomat. As it was, she had to be both, without quite seeming to be either.'

In May 2007, President George W. Bush winked at the Queen after mixing up his dates and referring to her visit to the White House in 1776 rather than 1976 for the American Bicentennial. The President later said that, 'She gave me a look only a mother could give a child.'

The 2007 royal visit was not the first time the Queen had met George Bush Junior. She found him and his wife Laura very easy to get along with, just as she had his parents. Hosting a thank-you dinner at the British Embassy towards the end of her trip, the Queen was adamant that President George Bush Senior and his wife Barbara should also be part of the line-up for the official photographs.

After dinner, the Queen began her speech, 'Mr President, I wondered whether I should start this toast saying, "When

I was here in 1776" ...' the room erupted. She went on to toast the 'strength and vitality' of the relationship between their two countries and raised a glass to all the Bushes and to 'enduring friendship'.

Barack and Michelle Obama first met the Queen and Prince Philip at Buckingham Palace in 2009 and went on to meet them on two more occasions. Photographs of the four show them smiling and looking relaxed. The world watched with bated breath when Mrs Obama put her arm around the Queen, but the Monarch seemed quite happy and the gesture was reciprocated. During the second visit in 2011, it was the President who made the mistake when he proposed a toast to Her Majesty and then proceeded to talk over the national anthem, later joking that the music was a soundtrack for his speech.

By the time of the third visit in 2016, relations were so relaxed that when the Queen and Prince Philip picked up the Obamas to drive them to lunch at Windsor Castle, the President immediately nipped in to sit in the front with Prince Philip. It was the First Lady's turn to hesitate, wary of offending royal protocol. 'Oh, it's all rubbish,' said the Queen, ushering her into the car. 'Just get in.'

A Great Brand

The latest incumbent of the White House is said to have committed several faux pas when meeting the Monarch during his visit to Britain in summer 2018. President Donald Trump was ten minutes late, shook the Queen's hand instead of bowing, walked in front of her and finally he turned his back on her.

The President called her a 'tremendous person', but was remarkably restrained on the subject of what they had discussed, saying instead, 'Let me tell you what I can talk about. She is an incredible woman, she is so sharp, she is so beautiful, when I say beautiful – inside and out. That is a beautiful woman.' And also: 'If you think of it, for so many years she has represented her country, she has really never made a mistake. You don't see, like, anything embarrassing. She is just an incredible woman.'

The Queen has remained diplomatically tight-lipped, at least in public and on the record, upon the subject of President Trump's state visit in June 2019. There was a flurry of contentious tweets from the President immediately before Air Force One touched down at Stansted Airport and some decidedly awkward comments about the Duchess of Sussex, but the general feeling was that there was nothing the veteran Monarch wouldn't be able to deal with.

At the state banquet at the end of the first day, the evening before the 75th D-Day commemorations began, the Queen's speech was thought to send a subtle message to President Trump, containing a gently veiled criticism of his policy: 'After the shared sacrifices of the Second World War, Britain and the United States worked with other allies to build an assembly of international institutions, to ensure that the horrors of conflict would never be repeated.'

However, in royal terms the visit appeared to pass off without any major lapses of protocol. The President's long-time friend, the CEO of Newsmax Media Christopher Ruddy, who also attended the banquet, said to the BBC's *Today* programme, 'The Trumps and Ivanka was there. Don Junior. – I spoke to them all last night – Jared. They were so impressed and these are folks not easily impressed. Remember they have their own ballrooms and palaces ... so they are used to very high living, sort of American Royalty, should we say.' He continued, 'The President has tremendous respect for not only the British royals but for Britain. This is a President that loves brands. The Queen has the greatest brand in the world, doesn't she? I think he is just super impressed by that.'

Entente Cordiale

Relations with the UK's closest neighbour are not always the closest, but the Queen has constantly played her part in keeping the relationship cordial.

In 1960, the Queen invited the French President Charles de Gaulle and his wife for a state visit. This was to be an extravagant stay, offering all the pomp and majesty that Britain could muster. It began with a ceremonial welcome. The Queen and President rode in an open-top landau carriage from London's Victoria Station to Buckingham Palace. The streets were packed with spectators to watch the procession roll past with mounted guard of honour and marching bands. Lunch with the Royal Family and a state banquet followed, alongside De Gaulle's address to parliament, a royal gala at Covent Garden opera house and a lavish firework display at the Palace. Afterwards, the French President wrote that he had found the Queen to be 'well informed about everything, that her judgements on people and events were as clear-cut as they were thoughtful, that no one was more preoccupied by the cares and problems of our storm-tossed age'.

The Queen has always been a popular figure with the French public. When she visited in 1948 as a newly married young Princess, crowds turned out to glimpse 'Zizette' as many French liked to call her. Sir Oliver Harvey, who was the British Ambassador at the time, reported back to the Foreign Office: 'It was an unusual experience to see the townsfolk of Paris cheer an English Princess from the Place de la Bastille.' Another former British Ambassador to France, Sir Christopher Mallaby, believes that 'the French think that monarchy is a splendid arrangement for other people, but not for themselves'. And the Queen has continued to be greeted warmly on her frequent visits to the country.

At Chantilly Racecourse in June 1974, where she had gone to watch her filly Highclere compete in (and ultimately win) the Prix de Diane, France's equivalent of The Oaks, the Queen was almost mobbed by racegoers shouting enthusiastically, '*Vive la reine!*' It took the combined efforts of her racing manager Lord Porchester, stud manager Sir Michael Oswald and a group of gendarmes to protect the Monarch from the crowd.

In May 1972, just seven months before Britain joined the EU (then the Common Market), the Queen visited France and summarized matters thus: 'We may drive on different sides of the road, but we're going the same way.' Both she and Prince Philip are fluent in French and often spoke the language on state visits, not requiring the services of an interpreter.

In June 2014, at a state banquet in Paris hosted by President François Hollande, Her Majesty again referred to the inimitable relationship of the two countries, talking in French of their 'friendship, good-humoured rivalry and admiration'. She also spoke of the Channel being 'not a line of partition, but a line of union', which made a rather neat pun in French as '*trait d'union*' (line of union) literally translates as 'hyphen'. At the time, the Queen was in France for the 70th anniversary of the D-Day landings, and as the last head of state to wear a uniform during the Second World War, when she arrived for the ceremony she was given a standing ovation by other heads of state. From the ordinary public and war veterans came the customary chorus of '*Vive la reine!*'

Annie Leibovitz's 2017 photographic portrait of the Queen broke normal rules by appearing on the front cover of French *Vanity Fair* alongside its British and US counterparts, which never usually happens. In France, it carried the admiring headline '*La reine du cool*'.

Uncharacteristically, the Queen nearly caused a diplomatic incident when she spoke in Koblenz in central Germany in May 1965. Her state visit was taking place just before the 150th anniversary of the Battle of Waterloo, the famous British victory over Napoleon Bonaparte and the French, in which the Duke of Wellington had been helped by the support of the Prussian Army. The Queen referred to the historic co-operation, going on to say, 'For fifty years, we heard too much about the things which have divided us. Let us now make a great effort to remember the things which unite us.'

The French were not impressed and outraged headlines appeared in a Paris newspaper referring to the Queen's 'monstrous gaffe'.

The Queen's visit to Germany, on the other hand, was an unqualified success, particularly her visit to Berlin and the Berlin Wall, which followed a series of diplomatic discussions about how much of the Wall the Queen could see without offending the Soviets. In the event, large numbers of East Berliners turned out hoping for a glimpse of Her Majesty and West Berliners, being from 'a beleaguered city ... felt particularly happy at being singled out for this special treat-ment'. The German newspaper *Bild* carried the headline, 'Your Majesty, you were wonderful.'

This was the first of many trips to Germany over the years, with several official visits as well as five state tours. In 1978, the Queen was again in Berlin at the Wall, declaring, 'My people stand behind you' to a large appreciative crowd. In 1992, she was there for the reunification of East and West Germany and also to attend a service honouring the civilian victims of the wartime Dresden bombing, at which a choir from Coventry Cathedral sang and Prince Philip read in German.

In 2015, the Queen was once more looking at past and present, meeting survivors and liberators of the Bergen-Belsen concentration camp. The then Prime Minister David Cameron was also there, and he commented, 'She is so loved in Germany. The crowds were off the charts. I was really struck by how many times she had been and how hard she worked on this relationship.' At the end of the Queen's 2015 visit, the *Bild* headline was, 'We love you, Ma'am'.

Historic Meetings

Meeting Russian President Boris Yeltsin at the Kremlin during her historic trip to Russia in 1994, the Queen said in her state banquet speech, 'You and I have spent most of our lives believing that this evening could never happen. I hope that you are as delighted as I am to be proved wrong.'

For his part, President Yeltsin toasted the Queen as a beacon of stability: 'In Russia, the Queen is seen as the personification of state wisdom, continuity of history, greatness of the nation. Bearing your mission with dignity, Your Majesty, you confirm an important idea: monarchy can be an integral part of a democratic system of government, an embodiment of the spiritual and historic unity of a nation.'

Boris Yeltsin was not the first Russian leader to be charmed by the Queen. At the height of the Cold War in 1956, the First Secretary of the Communist Party of the Soviet Union Nikita Khrushchev and his Prime Minister Nikolai Bulganin came to Britain for a state visit. Although they were not guests of the Queen, they were both very keen to meet her during their stay. They were invited to Windsor Castle, where the Queen and Prince Philip gave them a guided tour and served them Russian tea. Afterwards, President Khrushchev was won over, and said how impressed he had been that the Monarch 'had such a gentle, calm voice. She was completely unpretentious, completely without the haughtiness that you'd expect of royalty … In our eyes she was first and foremost the wife of her husband and the mother of her children.'

The Queen described setting foot on South African soil in March 1995 as 'one of the outstanding experiences of my life'. She was met by enthusiastic crowds and greeted by President Nelson Mandela, her host for the six-day state visit. The Queen had first met Mandela in 1991 at the Commonwealth Heads of Government Meeting in Zimbabwe. He and President Kenneth Kaunda of Zambia were the only two world leaders to address the Queen as 'Elizabeth' without causing offence.

When President Mandela arrived for his four-day state visit to Britain in July 1996, he was met by the Queen with a ceremonial welcome at Horse Guards Parade and the two were taken back to Buckingham Palace in one of Her Majesty's open-top carriages. Thousands stood by to watch and cheer as they rode past. At the state banquet given in his honour, the Queen paid tribute to the South African leader who 'has a special place in my heart and in the hearts of the British people'.

Breaking with tradition, instead of the usual state dinner to thank the Queen for her hospitality, President Mandela organized a party of music and dance at the Royal Albert Hall. Entitled 'Two Nations Celebrate', the evening was to raise funds for both The Prince's Trust and Mandela's Nations Trust for disadvantaged schoolchildren in South Africa, and well-known performers such as Quincy Jones, Phil Collins, Hugh Masekela and Ladysmith Black Mambazo were happy to take part. In the royal box President Mandela was soon on his feet dancing to the music. Prince Charles and Prince Philip, too, stood swaying and clapping. Then, to everyone's surprise, they were joined by the Queen, 'who has seldom been known to boogie in public' as the *Daily Telegraph* pointed out the following day.

Strained Relations

The Queen has also had to endure visits by some fairly questionable guests during her long reign, particularly during the 1970s. Among them were the despotic Ugandan President Idi Amin, who made state visits to the UK in 1971 and 1972. By 1977, the world knew about Amin's torture squads and brutal massacres of his own people. Yet, as the head of a Commonwealth country, the dictator could still have attended the Commonwealth Heads of Government Meeting held in Britain that year to coincide with the Silver Jubilee celebrations. Diplomatic pressure had been applied to dissuade him from coming, but Amin was unpredictable.

As guests assembled at St Paul's Cathedral for the Service of Thanksgiving marking the Queen's twenty-five years on the throne, no one actually knew whether the dictator would show up or not. Earl Mountbatten recorded in his diary that during the service the Queen had looked less than composed at times. He wrote, 'I asked her afterwards why she had looked rather cross and worried. She laughed and said, "I was just thinking how awful it would be if Amin were to gatecrash the party".' Mountbatten then asked what she would have done if he had, 'She had decided she would use the City's Pearl Sword, which the Lord Mayor had placed in front of her, to hit him hard over the head with.'

Privately, the Queen referred to Romanian dictator Nicolae Ceaușescu as 'that frightful little man', but diplomacy and duty meant that she had to put aside her personal feelings to lay on a full state welcome for the President and his wife in 1978.

To make matters worse, President Giscard d'Estaing of France warned the Queen of the bad conduct displayed by the dictator's entourage during a recent visit to Paris: 'The place had been wrecked … There were lots of lamps, vases, ashtrays and bathroom fittings. After their departure the place had been emptied. Everything had been unscrewed. It was as if burglars had moved in for a whole summer.' There were even holes in the walls where Romanian security had checked for hidden bugging devices.

By the time the Ceauşescus arrived in June, the government was already regretting its invitation and it very much fell to the Queen, Prince Philip and other members of the Royal Family to welcome and entertain the pair. The Foreign Secretary David Owen carefully omits any mention of the dictator's visit in his diaries, not entirely joking when he says, 'I try to pretend it never happened!'

It was not so easily forgotten by the Queen. Fifteen years later, when she made her own first state visit to Eastern Europe, she met John Birch, the British Ambassador to Hungary, who had worked in the Romanian capital Bucharest earlier in his diplomatic career. He recalled how 'she talked about the dreadful experience of having Ceauşescu to stay'.

Pineapples and Crocodiles

The Queen, along with other members of the Royal Family, has received some rather unusual gifts over the years and learned to accept all of them graciously and appreciatively – even when it's not totally apparent what the gift is or, more to the point, quite what she should do with it.

Joint wedding presents to Princess Elizabeth and Prince Philip in 1947 included 500 tins of pineapple, as well as crates of apples and bottles of sloe gin, while the hundreds of pairs of nylon stockings were obviously intended for the Princess alone. These were not such an odd gift for the time, as wartime rationing was still in place and stockings were in very short supply.

On official visits, the exchange of gifts is customary and can bring surprises. Aside from food, artworks, swords and ceremonial clubs, cowboy boots and hats have also featured. The 100-foot totem pole the Queen was gifted by the people of Canada in 1958 is now a feature of Windsor Great Park, while the Maori canoe that was a present from the government of New Zealand is on long-term loan to the British Museum.

In 1961, during a visit to The Gambia, the Queen presumably knew the ever-resourceful Martin Charteris (then her Assistant Private Secretary) would be up to the task when she asked him to look after a baby crocodile she had accepted as a gift for Prince Andrew. He kept the small but snappy reptile in his bathtub until a more suitable lodging could be found for it.

Living gifts can be harder to rehome and many of the more exotic animals have been taken in by London Zoo. President William Tubman of Liberia gave Prince Philip a pair of pygmy hippopotami, while in 1956, Soviet leaders Khrushchev and Bulganin presented six-year-old Princess Anne with a brown Syrian bear cub. Jaguars, black beavers, a pair of sloths, giant turtles, and an elephant named Jumbo, as well as many others, have all found new homes at the zoo.

Over the years, amongst the more unusual items, the Queen has been given a box of snail shells, Salt Island salt from the British Virgin Islands, soap to kill fleas, 7 kg of prawns (despite the fact that she is not a fan) and a grove of maple trees. She has also been offered horse sperm from a prize stallion.

6

Royal Etiquette

The Queen is a known traditionalist and is very aware of her family's unique position. She recognizes the dignity of her office and appreciates that there's a fine balance between appearing properly regal but also relatable. There still needs to be some magic and members of the public don't want royalty to be exactly like everyone else. For 'the Firm' there is always a right and wrong way of doing things, and royal protocol not only covers every aspect of behaviour but also extends to what they wear.

Dressing Like a Royal

Increasingly, the Queen's preferred formal dress for male family members on official business is being replaced, at least by the younger generation. Ties are being dropped in favour of a 'smart casual style' for daytime dressing. The Queen is thought to approve of the relaxing of royal protocol as long as the Princes adhere to formal attire for evening events or church services and more formal daytime duties. Nevertheless, the royal rules for dress still apply and like the generation before them, the Duchesses of Cambridge and Sussex still abide by many of the Queen's commands.

In the late sixties, when Mary Quant and
the mini skirt came to epitomize all that was
fashionable, Princess Anne suggested that
her mother might also consider shortening
her hemline. The Queen's response was
unequivocal: 'I am not a film star.'

The Queen's choice of clothing is also determined by practicality. Sleeves are never too long to avoid the danger of dipping into dishes of food at dinner or catching on a glass. They must also always allow easy movement. On one occasion, the Queen had to lift the ceremonial sword particularly high to knight an extremely tall man: 'I heard a ripping noise and my sleeve got torn. It was hard to know who was the most embarrassed.'

When Margaret Thatcher was Prime Minister she was mortified after arriving at a public ceremony with the Queen only to find they were dressed in similar outfits. To avoid this happening again, Mrs Thatcher sent a note to the Palace asking if she could be informed what the Queen would be wearing ahead of any joint engagements. The reply she received was dismissive: 'Do not worry. The Queen does not notice what other people are wearing.'

What are the Dos and Don'ts of Royal Dressing?

- If you're unmarried you're not allowed to wear a tiara. Also, tiaras should never be worn before 6 p.m. with a few notable exceptions, such as a royal wedding.

- There is a right and a wrong way to wear a tiara. The secret is that people should be able to see both your face and the jewels, and ideally it should be tilted at a 45-degree angle.

- For daytime events, hats are a must for women before 6 p.m., after which it's tiara time. This rule is increasingly being relaxed, but the Queen still expects a titfer (and not a fascinator) for formal occasions.

- Short skirts are frowned upon and hems should be no more than a couple of inches above the knee, otherwise it's short shrift from Her Majesty.

- To avoid over-exposure in a breeze, the Queen has small lead weights sewn into the hems of her skirts and dresses, a practical solution copied by the younger Princesses.

- Bare legs are another no-no. Even the newest member of the family, Meghan, the Duchess of Sussex, is conforming and wearing skin-coloured tights when on official duty. The Queen also disapproves of crossed legs; ankle crossing is fine, but better to have one's feet side by side. This is because legs and knees must be kept together. Kate, the Duchess of Cambridge, has perfected 'the duchess slant', a flattering pose favoured by Diana and now adopted by Meghan.

- Wedges are frowned upon. The Queen particularly dislikes this shoe style once beloved by Kate, which is now confined to appearances well away from her grandmother-in-law.

- As wife of an heir to the throne, Kate is expected to observe stricter standards than other members of the family, and it is likely that Meghan will be allowed a greater freedom.

- Strong bright colours are favoured by the Queen when choosing clothes, as she is always aware of her duty to be seen. She knows people have often travelled a long way, or waited for hours just to catch a glimpse of her, and muted shades would make Her Majesty hard to spot in a crowd. 'She needs to stand out for people to be able to say, "I saw the Queen",' her daughter-in-law Sophie

Wessex explained in the documentary *The Queen at 90*. Her Majesty herself said, 'If I wore beige, nobody would know who I am.' For the same reason, she is careful to use a transparent umbrella in the rain.

- The Queen also uses her famous Launer handbags to good effect to send subtle signals to her aides. When she wishes to end a conversation or needs rescuing, the bag is placed on the floor. If it's time to leave a dinner, the bag appears on the table – a regal version of a five-minute warning.

- For any royals who have served in the armed forces, military uniforms are to be worn at most formal events.

- Young Princes are expected to wear smart shorts, never trousers (which are far too middle class) until around the age of eight. Prince George follows the tradition, as did his father, uncle and grandfather.

- Coats should stay on. However warm it is, removing them in public is viewed as unladylike.

- The Queen favours black or white gloves for public meet-and-greets. They offer protection and help guard against the spread of germs.

- Subtle nails, practically manicured and varnished with a natural shade, are *de rigueur*. For her wedding to Prince Harry, Meghan chose the Queen's favourite Essie nail polish, 'Ballet Slippers'. Dark varnish is not allowed, though Kate stretches the rule by sporting red on her toes.

- A formal black outfit should always be to hand. This follows the young Queen's arrival back from Kenya in 1952, after her father's sudden death, when she was delayed for some time on the plane waiting for suitable mourning clothes to arrive from the Palace.

- Denim is not forbidden, though definitely not a favourite with 'the Firm': it's impossible to imagine the Queen in jeans. The general royal rule is that it is better to be over- rather than underdressed, so denim tends to be kept for private life – and never for the Monarch.

The Queen always carries her own umbrella, a practice that did not go unnoticed on a visit to Paris in 2014. It was June and the planned walkabout went ahead, despite the unseasonal rain. As usual the Monarch held her own umbrella. Meanwhile, her host Anne Hidalgo, the Parisian mayor, was accompanied by a staff member holding an umbrella to protect her from the downpour.

One peculiar perk of being the Sovereign is that the Queen has a servant who helps her to break in her shoes. It may sound extreme, but even at the age of ninety-three when most people would be taking life easy, the Queen still spends a lot of time standing or walking around at events. And if she's wearing a new pair of shoes, she can't complain of being uncomfortable or not able to walk any further. The sight of the Monarch kicking off her shoes and going barefoot to avoid blisters might also raise a few eyebrows in surprise. New shoes have to be immediately comfortable and wearable. As the Queen once commented drily, 'I'm used to standing. I have been standing all my life.'

Sir John Key, the former Prime Minister of New Zealand, once asked the Queen why she dressed formally when there were no crowds or photographers around. Her reply was simply, 'I am the last bastion of standards.'

All Change

For the press launch of her 'Back to Nature' garden at the 2019 Chelsea Flower Show, the Duchess of Cambridge was casually dressed in trousers and classic white Superga trainers. Prince William was also looking relaxed as he supported his wife in showcasing the garden she had designed to encourage families and children to 'get outside' and 'enjoy nature'.

A few hours later, and Kate had changed into a long floral Erdem dress, while William wore a formal navy suit and tie, ready to welcome the Queen for her evening visit before the garden opened to the public.

As Her Majesty walked up to the couple she smiled broadly and quipped, 'You're all looking very tidy.' Her grandson laughed, 'Well, I've smartened up.' Kate then took the Queen on a personal tour of the garden, which included a treehouse and rope swing, waterfall, rustic den and campfire.

A Handbag

Her Majesty is rarely seen without one of her signature Launer handbags. She is said to own more than 200 of them, with the appropriately named Royale and black patent Traviata being her favourites. The question of what exactly is inside the royal bag has been the subject of much debate.

She has no need for a passport or bank card, and the Queen famously never carries cash, apart from a crisp five- or ten-pound note for the church collection.

One long-serving member of staff described her boss as 'a very practical, down-to-earth lady', and so the contents of her handbag usually include reading glasses, tissues, mints and a fountain pen, along with a comb, lipstick and small mirror. The ever-prepared Monarch also carries a portable hook, in order that she can discreetly hang her handbag under the table when dining.

Incidentally, the Queen has been known to reapply her lipstick while sitting at the table and has been photographed doing so at the occasional sporting event. When former First Lady Barbara Bush was questioned about the etiquette of checking her lipstick in public at a Washington ladies' lunch, she replied, 'The Queen told me it was all right to do it.'

Luisa Mattioli, third wife of the actor Sir Roger Moore, was puzzled as to why the Queen carried her handbag with her inside Buckingham Palace. Her Majesty's answer was straightforward: 'This house is very big, you know.'

Table Matters

From how to hold a knife and fork (never on any account like a pencil – the handles are not made to be seen and should be politely covered at all times when eating) to how to tackle fruit, there is a royal right way to do it.

According to Princess Diana's former butler Paul Burrell, who first worked at Buckingham Palace as a footman, the Queen would never dream of peeling or eating a banana with her fingers. During an appearance on *Through the Keyhole*, Burrell demonstrated how Her Majesty neatly slices off the two ends with a knife, before cutting the length of the skin.

He explained: 'You split open the belly, some people eat it like a monkey of course … [the majority, surely?] Now you cut it up into small bite-size pieces and then you eat it … with your knife and fork.'

It has to be said that there is something pleasingly dextrous about completing the task (tested in the interests of research), as sliced banana somehow takes on a whole different texture.

The Royal Family apply a similar approach to most fruit, although not all should be peeled. When the actor David Suchet asked for advice on the correct way to peel a mango at lunch in 'polite company', Prince Philip revealed that 'you don't peel a mango, you slice it', before going on to demonstrate the royal technique.

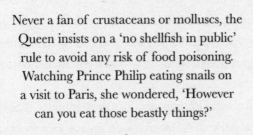

Never a fan of crustaceans or molluscs, the
Queen insists on a 'no shellfish in public'
rule to avoid any risk of food poisoning.
Watching Prince Philip eating snails on
a visit to Paris, she wondered, 'However
can you eat those beastly things?'

Royal etiquette dictates that no one should begin eating
before the Queen at a formal dinner, nor continue eating
after she has finished. Timings are important, too. The
Queen expects dinner to begin promptly at 8.30 p.m. and
houseguests should not retire to bed ahead of Her Majesty.

Utensils do the talking if you have to leave the table –
though who would dare? If you haven't finished eating, the
knife and fork should be crossed and left at the top of the
plate. Otherwise, if finished, they should be placed together
at a slight angle at the bottom of your plate.

In case you ever find yourself at a royal garden party, it might be useful to know that there's a right royal way to hold a teacup. Cup handles should be lightly held at the top using the thumb and index finger, with the rest of the fingers tucked under the handle supporting the cup. There should be no raising of pinkies and do make sure to sip from the same spot to avoid multiple lipstick stains.

The same goes for napkins. 'They're doing it all wrong,' the Queen once said to another dinner guest, indicating fellow diners at the long, formally set table who had their napkins the wrong way round on their laps. 'They've got the starched side down. The napkin will slip off their knees. You do it like this – the unstarched side on your lap and then you tuck it under your bottom.'

Protocol Dictates

Being royal brings multiple perks and privileges, but there are also some rules that the rest of us never have to think about. They're not set in stone, but the royals tend to toe the line.

- Members of the Royal Family don't sign autographs, in order to avoid the risk of forgery.

- There are no selfies. The Queen is said to find the mass of people trying to take selfies with her 'disconcerting' and 'strange', confessing to US Ambassador Matthew Barzun that it's odd for her when people stare at their screens instead of at her. Surprisingly, the Queen has been known to photo-bomb other people's selfies, and even a BBC news broadcast.

- The royals take a professional approach to public displays of affection. Often when out and about, couples are 'at work', and Prince William and Kate tend to follow the Queen and Prince Philip's example, showing their obvious affection in shared smiles, jokes and private asides. Prince Harry and Meghan are notably more openly affectionate and tactile in public.

- Senior members of the Royal Family must ask Her Majesty's permission to marry. Both Prince William and Prince Harry spoke to their grandmother before popping the question. An official letter granting consent is required by the Royal Marriages Act of 1772.

- The Queen traditionally spends Christmas at Sandringham where close family members are invited. However serious the relationship, only engaged or married partners are included.

- The Queen's permission must also be given for her heirs to fly together, perhaps due to her own well-hidden fear of flying?

- When meeting a member of the Royal Family, men are expected to bow while women curtsey. The secret is to be subtle. The bow or curtsey should not be flamboyant, though they should be held longer if meeting the Queen rather than another royal.

- The last person the Queen curtseyed to was her father George VI, and she is said to be very relaxed about curtseying, commenting that it is 'not necessarily right for modern times'.

- There is a strict order of precedence for bowing and curtseying and also for entering a room. The Queen comes first, naturally, followed by Prince Philip, then Prince Charles and Camilla, next Prince William and Kate, Prince Harry and Meghan, then the 'Blood Princesses', Anne, Beatrice and Eugenie. If Kate and Meghan are not accompanied by their husbands, they slip down the line and should curtsey to, or follow after, the Princesses by blood.

- When the Queen enters a room, everyone must stand because she is never off-duty. The rule even applies to

Prince Philip, although it's presumably relaxed when they're alone.

- When visitors are leaving the Queen's presence they used to have to walk backwards – the rule being to never turn your back on the Monarch. Health and safety in modern times has done away with this requirement, except for a few ceremonial occasions.

- The Queen should first be addressed as 'Your Majesty' and afterwards as 'Ma'am' (to rhyme with jam), though it's back to 'Your Majesty' when she is leaving.

- With definite echoes of Queen Victoria, royals should always descend a staircase gracefully with chin held parallel to the ground and hands down at their sides.

A Matter of Manners

When meeting the Queen, never mind protocol it's just plain bad manners to barge in.

Arriving late for a reception at Buckingham Palace, a guest realized he had missed his allotted place in the line of diplomats who were waiting to be introduced to the Queen. Determined not to pass up the opportunity to share a few words with the Sovereign, he pushed in among the others still awaiting their turn. When the Queen finally reached him, he was greeted with a cold hard stare and the strong arms of officials who escorted him away. He should have understood that upsetting the time-honoured British tradition of orderly queuing would fail to impress.

The guest who tried to muscle into a conversation at a reception for 350 prominent Americans in 2007 was given similarly short shrift. The Queen was talking to a group of sportsmen about football when their talk was interrupted by an interloper.

'Do you play football?' the Queen asked.

'No – I sell pancake and waffle mix,' the newcomer answered.

The Queen shook her head before turning away. 'How interesting what people will eat,' she remarked, in a tone loaded with irony.

Safety Conscious

When President Ronald Reagan and his wife Nancy visited the UK in 1982, a state banquet was held in their honour at Windsor Castle. After the dinner, in line with royal protocol, the Queen and the President left first. Other guests stood with their chairs pushed back to watch the two heads of state process from the banqueting hall, making their way between the rows of tables and chairs. They were led by the Lord Chamberlain Charles Maclean, who walked backwards facing the Queen as this was a formal ceremonial occasion. President Reagan noticed that the Queen was subtly signalling to the Lord Chamberlain, indicating right or left with her hand. She explained, 'We don't get those chairs even and he could fall over one and hurt himself.'

The Queen came to know the crew members on the Royal Yacht *Britannia* personally and developed a real rapport with them all, but the relaxed atmosphere on board was never applied to safety. Former Commander of the Yacht Sir Robert Woodard explained the Monarch's natural concern for the staff: 'If the Queen saw a Yachtsman working over the side without a lifejacket on, I was the first to know. Anything that risked life or limb would need immediate sorting out. She wouldn't remonstrate. She'd just say: "Quick, quick, there's someone without a lifejacket." She got to know them extremely well.'

Welcome Guests

The Queen certainly favours the personal touch. When expecting overnight guests, she always inspects their rooms herself – whether visitors are officials or family. Mary Wilson, wife of Prime Minister Harold Wilson, stayed at Balmoral several times during the 1970s and described their warm welcome: 'We went into the hall, and the Queen and Prince Philip came to greet us. There were bowls on the floor and corgis running around, and she put a vase of gentians in my room. The lady-in-waiting said the Queen thought I might like those. She gave a lot of thought to things like that.'

The Duchess of Cambridge revealed that when the Queen's great-grandchildren stay over, Her Majesty always leaves a small gift for them to find in their bedrooms. She also oversees the arrangements for banquets and official dinners, and has a keen eye for detail. However, once through the door some guests feel so at home that they show no inclination to leave. The Royal Family have developed a code to chivvy along anyone showing signs of outstaying their welcome. They will call for a butler and enquire if the guest's car has arrived. The butler then goes to 'check', returning with news that the car is indeed waiting.

Hands Off Her Majesty

No one is supposed to touch the Queen. If she offers a hand it is polite to take it, but only for the briefest of touches rather than a full-on handshake. Over the years there have been some very public breaches of this rule.

The Queen and Prince Philip formally met US President Barack Obama and his wife Michelle at Buckingham Palace in 2009, when the President was over for the G20 Summit in London. Gifts were exchanged, royal etiquette observed. Later, at the evening reception for world leaders, Mrs Obama was photographed breaking the code and hugging Her Majesty. More surprisingly, the Queen reciprocated with an affectionate arm around the First Lady's waist. The pair had been chatting together, apparently comparing shoes and height. At 5 feet 11 inches Michelle towered over the Queen, who at her peak was 5 feet 4 inches but has in all likelihood shrunk a little with the years.

In her memoir *Becoming*, Michelle Obama explained that the Queen looked down at the black Jimmy Choos the First Lady was wearing and then shook her head. Pointing down at her own black pumps, Her Majesty remarked, 'These shoes are unpleasant, are they not?' Mrs Obama wrote: 'I confessed then to the Queen that my feet were hurting. She confessed that hers hurt, too. We looked at each other then with identical expressions, like, when is all this standing around with world leaders going to finally wrap up? And with this, she busted out with a fully charming laugh.'

After the photographs appeared, a Buckingham Palace spokesperson denied there had been a breach of protocol, explaining, 'It was a mutual and spontaneous display of affection. We don't issue instructions on not touching the Queen.'

The 2009 meeting with the Obamas was actually not the first time the Monarch had been publicly hugged. In a visit to Washington, D.C. in 1991, great-grandmother Alice Frazier hugged the smiling Queen warmly when the Sovereign visited her home, saying it just felt like the natural thing to do: 'It's the American way. I couldn't stop myself.'

During a surge in the crowd at one Royal walkabout, *Daily Express* photographer Victor Blackman almost lost his balance, and in an attempt to stop himself falling he grabbed the Queen. He apologized profusely, but the Queen was unruffled. 'Not your fault, Mr Blackman. It will give you something to write about if you ever write your memoirs.'

When the Australian Prime Minister Paul Keating dared to put his arm around the Queen when she visited in 1992, it caused an uproar. The tabloids dubbed him the 'Lizard of Oz'. When his successor John Howard was accused of repeating the mistake, his office was swift to quash the story and issued a statement, saying, 'We firmly deny that there was any contact whatsoever.' Close press scrutiny of photographs showed that indeed there was no contact. Howard's arm hovered in mid-air a few centimetres away from the royal back.

The *entente cordiale* with France got a little too cordial in 2004, when President Jacques Chirac guided the Queen as they walked the streets of Paris, grasping her arm and touching her shoulder and back. This time it was the *Daily Mail* that complained, headlining its article 'Hands Off!'

And in 2017, the Governor of Canada David Johnston felt it necessary to provide a public explanation after he was seen touching the Queen's elbow during Canada's 150th anniversary celebrations at Canada House in London: 'I'm certainly conscious of the protocol. I was just anxious to be sure there was no stumbling on the steps. It's a little bit awkward, that descent to Trafalgar Square, and there was carpet that was a little slippy, so I thought perhaps it was appropriate to breach protocol just to be sure there was no stumble.'

The Royal Yacht *Britannia* was known for its informality, and over the many years of service it saw its share of royal high jinks and fun. But there were limits. During a very relaxed beach barbecue on a 1970 tour of Australia, guests decided it was time to swim. John Gorton, the former Prime Minister of Australia, recalled, 'Princess Anne was thrown in and then Prince Philip. I was sitting next to Her Majesty and I was just about to throw her in, but I looked at her and something about the way she looked at me told me that perhaps I shouldn't. In the end, the Queen was the only one who stayed dry.'

7

Wit and Wisdom

The standard image of Elizabeth II is one of dignity and authority. She is simply 'the Queen', the embodiment of royalty. Those who know her well, or who meet with her regularly, soon come to value her wealth of knowledge and experience, her considered replies. Most are also struck by her warmth and the dry wit that underlies many of her responses, although there is always a suspicion that many of her best lines are said off-camera, reserved for a trusted inner circle of family and friends.

When an MP commented that it must be a strain meeting so many strangers all the time, the Queen smiled and said, 'It is not as difficult as it might seem. You see, I don't have to introduce myself. They all seem to know who I am.'

Although, somewhat surprisingly, this is not always the case. And sometimes even the Monarch can pass unrecognized, especially when running her own errands out of the city and away from official engagements. Stopped by a fellow shopper in the village grocers in Sandringham, the Queen was told, 'You *do* look like the Queen.'

Smiling in response, Her Majesty answered, 'How very reassuring.'

Similarly incognito in the Highlands of Scotland, the Queen was out walking close to her Balmoral Estate, dressed for the weather in a heavy tweed coat and headscarf. While accompanied by her former police protection officer Richard Griffin, she was approached by some American tourists who asked if she lived in the area. The Queen answered simply that she had a house nearby. At this point the group asked if she had ever met the Queen. 'No,' she replied, before pointing at her protection officer, 'but he has.' The group left, none the wiser.

Queen of All

Over the decades the Queen has remained reluctant to pass comment in public or in the press, her maxim of 'never complain, never explain' having served her well. It's thought that she tries to encourage the rest of her family to follow her unofficial doctrine of 'don't say much at all' – but with rather mixed success.

With family and trusted friends it is a different matter. And, like most people, Her Majesty loves to know what's going on with everyone, admitting, 'A good gossip is a wonderful tonic.'

Her son Prince Andrew once commented, 'The Queen's intelligence network is a hell of a lot better than anyone's in this Palace. Bar none. She knows everything. I don't know how she does it. And she sees everything.' He also said, 'Sarah will talk to me about someone and I don't know who she's talking about, but if she talks to my mother, the two of them will know exactly – and across several generations, too.'

A senior member of the Royal Household backed up this opinion in 2011, observing, 'Well … she knows what's going on. She had a good nose for a story. She would have been a good journalist.'

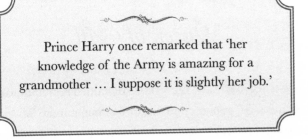

Prince Harry once remarked that 'her knowledge of the Army is amazing for a grandmother … I suppose it is slightly her job.'

At the end of a day on board the Royal Yacht *Britannia*, Queen Elizabeth II liked nothing better than to relax, kick off her shoes (quite literally) and chat about the day's events and visitors. The staff remember fondly the laughter and teasing that always accompanied the gossip, as well as the fact that their Sovereign 'didn't miss a thing'.

The Queen got to know crew members very well over the years and trusted them implicitly. At the start of a voyage, after a gap of time, she would always ask after them and their families, remembering names and details. The Royal Yacht gave the Queen and other family members the chance to behave normally away from the public eye and camera lenses.

Stormy Waters

Susan Crosland, widow of former Foreign Secretary Anthony Crosland, recalled their time on board the Royal Yacht in 1976, during a state visit to mark the American Bicentennial: 'On one occasion when Philip was sounding off about something, the Queen said to him quite sharply, "Oh, Philip, do shut up. You don't know what you're talking about."'

The trip had been beset by storms and when *Britannia* ran into a force 9 gale en route to Philadelphia from Bermuda, most of those on board were struck down with seasickness. Not Her Majesty. After dinner that evening, the Queen stood up and attempted to open the sliding door of the dining room. She grasped the handle as the Yacht jolted violently in the swell. With her back pressed to the door, the Queen moved with the door as it slowly shut.

'Wheee!' the Monarch laughed, repeating it as she swung back and forth before finally managing to slip through a narrow gap and then merrily calling out 'Goodnight!' before the door closed again.

In calmer seas the next morning, everyone was feeling much better. 'I have never seen so many grim and grey faces around a dinner table,' the Queen joked. 'Philip was not at all well ... I'm glad to say.'

> Early in her reign, Harold Macmillan, her third Prime Minister, said of the young Queen, 'She does not enjoy "society". She likes her horses. But she loves her duty and means to be a queen and not a puppet.'

Politics and the Palace

As Head of State the Queen is expected to remain strictly neutral with respect to political matters. As the UK Parliament website states, 'Although not prohibited by law, it is considered unconstitutional for the Monarch to vote in an election.'

So far, fifteen Prime Ministers have served Queen Elizabeth II since her accession in 1952 and all have come to value her calm authority, wisdom and knowledge. She meets with them regularly once a week in the evening at

Buckingham Palace to discuss current affairs of state. When her children were small, she requested that the meeting be held later to give her time to read the children their bedtime story first.

Asked which Prime Minister's weekly evening meetings she had most enjoyed, the Queen had no hesitation. 'Winston, of course, because it was always such fun.'

Churchill's daughter Mary Soames reckoned their discussions often veered away from the political, saying, 'They spent a lot of the audience talking about horses.' Sir Alan 'Tommy' Lascelles, who was Private Secretary to the Queen from 1952 to 1953, wrote about their meetings in his diary: 'I could not hear what they talked about, but it was, more often than not, punctuated by peals of laughter, and Winston generally came out wiping his eyes. "She's *en grande beauté ce soir*," he said one evening, in his schoolboy French.'

Mary Soames described the relationship between the young Sovereign and elderly statesman: '[The Queen] was very well versed in her constitutional position. My father knew very well what the position of constitutional monarch is *vis-à-vis* prime minister, cabinet and parliament. So it was a great advantage for her first prime minister to be somebody who really did know that … They talked about the present. They must have talked about people. Young though she was, she had experience. She travelled. She probably knew some of the people better than he, so she would have told him about them. What struck my father was her attentiveness.

She has always paid attention to what she was doing. He never said she was lacking confidence.'

No records are ever kept of the Monarch and Prime Minister's discussions and no one else is present apart from the Queen's constant companions, her corgis. John Major, PM from 1990 to 1997, joked about the dogs, 'If they were bugged, all our state secrets would be apparent.'

It is always maintained that the Queen never favours one politician or party over another. The former Clerk of the Privy Council Sir Godfrey Agnew claimed, 'The Queen doesn't make fine distinctions between politicians of different parties. They all roughly belong to the same social category in her view.'

Martin Charteris, the Private Secretary who probably knew the Queen best of all since he worked for her in the days when she was still Princess Elizabeth, told historian Peter Hennessy, 'You might say that the Queen prefers a sort of consensus politics, rather than a polarized one, and I suspect this is true, although I can't really speak from knowledge here. But if you are in the Queen's position, you are the titular, the symbolic head of the country, and the less squabbling that goes on in that country, obviously the more convenient and the more comfortable you feel.'

On his relationship with the Queen, James Callaghan (PM from 1976 to 1979) concluded, 'What one gets is friendliness not friendship.'

Edward Heath came to value his weekly audiences with the Monarch in the early 1970s: 'It was always a relief to be able to discuss everything with someone, knowing full well that there was not the slightest danger of anything leaking.' As a result, during his time as Prime Minister he would not only talk about politics but a range of topics, including Northern Ireland, the personal affairs of other politicians and world leaders, and his attempts to 'join Europe'.

Another senior politician remarked, 'There's a lot of nonsense talked about what a terrible life she has. Nonsense! I think she loves it.'

The Queen was an old hand by the time Margaret Thatcher took over at Number 10, leading the Iron Lady to comment, 'I do not think anyone fully realizes the accumulation of experience she has.'

There was said to be a certain 'stiffness' between the two powerful women, at least in the early days. The Queen found her first female Prime Minister too deferential – no one could curtsey lower than Margaret Thatcher, who generally tried too hard. A friend admitted, 'The Queen had some most amusing and well-observed lines about Thatcher.'

One was a joke about a visit to a nursing home where the Prime Minister tried chatting to an elderly resident. The Queen would perfectly imitate Mrs Thatcher's rather strident tone asking, 'Do you know who I am?' whereupon the resident replied, 'No, but if you ask the nurse, she'll tell you.'

It is a tradition that the current Prime Minister and spouse always visit the Queen during her summer stay at Balmoral. On the second evening there would be a barbecue organized by Prince Philip. Mrs Thatcher is said to have found the whole event somewhat odd, but was particularly shocked to see the Sovereign helping to clear up afterwards and, worse still, washing up with bare hands. After one visit, Mrs Thatcher sent the Queen a pair of rubber gloves, on another she kept trying to help, succeeding only in getting in the way. Finally, the Queen hissed through gritted teeth, 'Will somebody please tell that woman to sit down?'

Despite their different characters, by the end of Margaret Thatcher's eleven years as PM the Queen had come to respect her premier. A former adviser to the Crown reflected, 'As someone who inherited her position, she is interested in meritocrats.' After their weekly evening meetings, Mrs T was often asked to stay on for a whisky or two with the Queen, and a senior official at the Palace remembered how animated the conversations between the pair were. After Mrs Thatcher retired, one of the Queen's courtiers hosted a lunch for the Monarch and former premier, commenting, 'The Queen was much more fond of Margaret than I realized, though amused by her.'

During John Major's time as Prime Minister, he hosted a dinner for the Queen to which several former PMs were invited. Among them was Edward Heath, who by then was almost eighty years old and in increasingly frail health. As the most senior politician present he was seated next to the Queen, but had trouble keeping awake during the lengthy meal. At one point, John Major pointed out, 'Ted's fallen asleep.' The Queen smiled, 'I know he has, but don't worry. He'll wake up a little later and we'll say nothing about it.'

When Tony Blair first arrived at Buckingham Palace after his election win in May 1997, he stepped forward and tripped, almost grabbing the Monarch's hand in a bid to steady himself. He was just forty-three, the youngest Prime Minister that Britain had had since 1812, and the Queen appeared kindly oblivious to his stumble. To put him at ease, she explained that he was her tenth PM, 'The first was Winston. That was before you were born.'

She was less impressed with Tony Blair's 'Cool Britannia' campaign, which saw a wave of youthful artists invited to Downing Street. The Queen commented to her cousin Margaret Rhodes, 'Poor Britannia. She would have hated being cool.'

Blair called the Queen 'a symbol of unity in a world of insecurity … simply the best of British'. He went on to publish his memoirs in 2010, in which he revealed some of the details of his conversations with the Queen. She was said to be 'deeply disappointed' and it is perhaps significant that he has not received a knighthood since leaving office.

Now a veteran of the weekly meetings with her Prime Ministers, the Queen herself has said of them, 'They unburden themselves ... It's rather nice to feel that one's a sort of sponge.' She has also confessed that when listening, 'Some things stay there and some things go out the other ear.'

Prince Philip's verdict on his wife's role is that 'because she's the Sovereign everyone turns to her. If you have a King and a Queen, there are certain things people automatically go to the Queen about. But if the Queen is also *The Queen*, they go to her about everything. She's asked to do much more than she would normally do.'

Bibliography

Airlie, Mabell, *Thatched with Gold: The Memoirs of Mabell, Countess of Airlie* (Hutchinson, 1962)

Arscott, David, *Queen Elizabeth II, Diamond Jubilee, 60 Years a Queen: A Very Peculiar History* (Book House, 2012)

Balding, Ian, *Making the Running: A Racing Life* (Headline, 2005)

Bedell Smith, Sally, *Elizabeth the Queen: The Life of a Modern Monarch* (Penguin Random House, 2012)

Blair, Tony, *A Journey* (Hutchinson, 2010)

Botham, Noel and Montague, Bruce, *The Book of Royal Useless Information* (John Blake Publishing, 2012)

Bradford, Sarah, *Elizabeth: A Biography of Her Majesty the Queen* (Booksales, 2002)

Brandreth, Gyles, *Philip and Elizabeth: Portrait of a Marriage* (Arrow Books, 2004)

Burrell, Paul, *A Royal Duty* (Penguin, 2004)

Carey, George, *Know the Truth: A Memoir* (HarperCollins Publishers, 2004)

Churchill, Winston and Churchill, Clementine, *Speaking for Themselves: The Personal Letters of Winston and Clementine Churchill*, ed. Mary Soames (Black Swan, 1999)

Clarke, Stephen, *Elizabeth II: Queen of Laughs* (Stephen Clarke, 2018)

Crawford, Marion, *The Little Princesses* (Orion, 2003)

Crosland, Susan, *Tony Crosland* (Jonathan Cape, 1982)

Crossman, Richard, *The Crossman Diaries*, ed. Anthony Howard (Hamish Hamilton/Jonathan Cape, 1976)

Dampier, Phil and Walton, Ashley, *What's in the Queen's Handbag and Other Royal Secrets* (Book Guild Publishing, 2007)

Dolby, Karen, *The Wicked Wit of Queen Elizabeth II* (Michael O'Mara Books, 2015)

Hardman, Robert, *Monarchy: The Royal Family at Work* (Ebury, 2007)

Hardman, Robert, *Queen of the World* (Century, 2018)

Heald, Tim, *The Duke: A Portrait of Prince Philip* (Hodder & Stoughton, 1991)

Hennessy, Peter, *Having it So Good: Britain in the Fifties* (Allen Lane, 2006)

Hoey, Brian, *At Home with the Queen: The Inside Story of the Royal Household* (HarperCollins, 2002)

Hoey, Brian, *Not in Front of the Corgis: Secrets of Life Behind the Royal Curtains* (The Robson Press, 2011)

Johnstone-Bryden, Richard, *The Royal Yacht* Britannia: *The Official History* (Conway Maritime Press, 2003)

Junor, Penny, *The Firm: The Troubled Life of the House of Windsor* (HarperCollins, 2011)

Lacey, Robert, *Royal: Her Majesty Queen Elizabeth II* (Little Brown, 2002)

Lascelles, Sir Alan, *King's Counsellor: Abdication and War: The Diaries of Sir Alan Lascelles*, ed. Duff Hart-Davis (Phoenix, 2007)

Leibovitz, Annie, *At Work* (Phaidon Press, 2018)

Longford, Elizabeth, *Elizabeth R: A Biography* (Weidenfeld & Nicolson, 1983)

Major, John, *The Autobiography* (HarperCollins, 1999)

Marr, Andrew, *The Diamond Queen: Elizabeth II and Her People* (Macmillan UK, 2011)

Moore, Charles, *Margaret Thatcher: The Authorized Biography, Volumes One and Two* (Allen Lane, 2013 and 2015)

Muscat, Julian, *Her Majesty's Pleasure: How Horseracing Enthrals the Queen* (Racing Post Books, 2012)

Obama, Michelle, *Becoming* (Viking, 2018)

Parker, Michael, *It's All Going Terribly Wrong: The Accidental Showman* (Benefactum Publishing, 2013)

Petrella, Kate, *Royal Wisdom: The Most Daft, Cheeky and Brilliant Quotes from Britain's Royal Family* (Adams Media, 2011)

Pimlott, Ben, *The Queen: Elizabeth II and the Monarchy* (HarperPress, 2012)

Reagan, Ronald, *The Reagan Diaries* (HarperCollins, New York, 2007)

Rhodes, Margaret, *The Final Curtsey: A Royal Memoir by the Queen's Cousin* (Birlinn Ltd and Umbria Press, 2012)

Roberts, Monty, *The Man Who Listens to Horses* (Hutchinson, 1996)

Seward, Ingrid, *My Husband and I: The Inside Story of 70 Years of the Royal Marriage* (Simon and Schuster, 2017)

Sinclair, Marianne and Litvinoff, Sarah (ed.), *The Wit and Wisdom of the Royal Family: A Book of Royal Quotes* (Plexus Publishing, 1990)

www.allgreatquotes.com

www.bbc.co.uk

www.biography.com

www.brainyquote.com

www.britroyals.com

www.dailymail.co.uk

www.express.co.uk

www.facebook.com/TheBritishMonarchy

www.famousquotesandauthors.com

www.guardian.co.uk

www.hellomagazine.com

www.huffingtonpost.com

www.independent.co.uk

www.inews.co.uk

www.itv.com

www.majestymagazine.co.uk

www.mirror.co.uk

www.news.sky.com/uk
www.nytimes.com
www.radiotimes.com
uk.reuters.com
www.royal.uk
www.royal.gov.uk
www.saidwhat.co.uk
www.scotsman.com
www.telegraph.co.uk
www.thesun.co.uk
www.thetimes.co.uk
www.thinkexist.com
www.time.com
www.timesonline.co.uk
www.trueroyalty.tv
www.vanityfair.com
www.vice.com
www.vox.com
en.wikipedia.org
www.yorkshirepost.co.uk

Picture Credits